York Street

The Story of Cheetham Hill Road

Martin Gittins

Copyright © Martin Gittins 2021

Email conduitzzz@outlook.com
Website www.all-things-considered.org
Please direct all enquiries to the author

The rights of Martin Gittins to be identified as the Author of this work has been asserted in accordance with the Copyrights, Designs and Patents Act 1988

ISBN 978-1-83853-994-1

First Published 2021
Independent Publishing Network

All rights reserved. No part of this book may be reprinted or reproduced or utilised in any form by any electronic, mechanical, or other means, now known or hereafter invented, including photocopying and recording, or in any information storage or retrieval system, without the permission in writing from the Publishers.

A British Library record for this book is available from the British Library.

York Street

CONTENTS

CHAPTER I - ROMAN TIMES – Page 1
Roman Manchester – Town and Fort – Temple – Bignor Roman Villa – Roman Altar

CHAPTER II - A LEISURELY STROLL – Page 5
Strangeways Park – Archibald Prentice – Gibraltar and Scotland – Wilton Terrace – Job's Stile Path
Eagle and Child Tavern – Felix Mendelssohn – C. W. Ethelston – Crumpsall Hall
Pilkington's Bow and Arrow Shop

CHAPTER III – SOME NOTABLE RESIDENTS AND VISITORS – Page 10
The Grant Brothers – Jack Rosenthal – Howard Jacobsen – Frances Hodgson Burnett
Benny Rothman – James Rawson – Joseph Hyman – James Crossley

CHAPTER IV – HOUSES AND BUILDINGS OF DISTINCTION – Page 24
Cheetham Town Hall - Cheetham Assembly Rooms – Prestwich Union Offices – Synagogues
Manchester Union Workhouse – Freed Library and Reading Room – Northern Hospital
Cheetham Baths Jewish Museum – Rosen Hallas – Ryecroft House – Sticks House – Temple Square
Queens Road Bus and Tram Depot – Crumpsall District Library – Joseph Holt's Brewery

CHAPTER V – SMEDLEY, THE FORGOTTEN SUBURB – Page 36
Beech Hill – Smedley Hill – Edward Chippindall – Stowell Manor – Smedley Bank
William Harrison Ainsworth – George Condy – John Rylands – Eustratio Ralli
Nathan Laski – Smedley House

CHAPTER VI – PLACES OF WORSHIP AND EDUCATION - Page 51
St. Mark's – St. Luke's – Temple School – St. Chad's – Notre Dame Convent – Victoria Wesleyan
Ducie Wesleyan Chapel – St. Mary's Ukrainian Catholic Church – Cheetham Hill Wesleyan Methodist
Trinity United – Heath Street School – The Khizra Mashjid – The North Manchester Jamia Mosque
Rosen Hallas School – Early Jewish Schools – King David School
Spanish and Portuguese Synagogue – Older Synagogues

CHAPTER VII – ENTERTAINMENT AND LEISURE – Page 67
The Griffin – The Temple – The Crumpsall – The George – The Half Way House – The Robin Hood
The Derby Brewery Arms – The Empress – The Pleasant – Ukrainian Clubs – The Polish Club
Premier Cinemas – Temperance Billiard Hall – The Temple Pictorium – The Odeon – The Globe
The Shakespeare – The Bijou – The Majestic Skating Rink – Finnigan's Dance Academy
The Ice Palace – Cheetham Wakes

CHAPTER VIII – MISCELLANY – Page 81
Cheetwood Urban Village - Car Showrooms – Police Station – Hotels
Books featuring Cheetham Hill – The Monkey Run

York Street

INTRODUCTION

Cheetham is a very old district, having been in existence since before the 14th century. The old village of was at the bottom of the hill and its ending in ham could well signify it as being an early Anglian colony (ceddeham-cedde being the Saxon word for a home), the literal translation of Cheetham meaning 'The Home by the Wood'.

In November 1906 the historian and author, Thomas Swindells, from Monton Green, Eccles, published the first of what was to become, over the next 2 years, a set of five volumes entitled 'Manchester Streets and Manchester Men.'

Since then, these books have become a valuable source of historical information for generations of researchers, historians and anyone with an interest in the local history of Manchester.

It is no surprise that, having dealt with the city centre itself in great detail, the majority of the remaining content of these five volumes concerns itself with areas to the north of the city centre, as it was here where the greatest outward expansion had taken place in the previous several hundred years.

This book proposes to walk in the footsteps of T. Swindells and explore again the byways of North Manchester York Street, better known to recent generations as Cheetham Hill Road.

From Victoria Station to its junction with Middleton Road at the Half Way House, Cheetham Hill Road measures some three and a half miles in length. Within that short distance is laid out some of the most significant history in the making of Manchester.

In reading the story of Cheetham Hill Road one will encounter great inventors, authors and musicians; men of business and enterprise; political and social reformers; ordinary and extraordinary folk; fighters for freedom and justice; and as rich a mix of nationalities and religions as could be found anywhere in the world.

Its public buildings have witnessed historic meetings and life-changing decisions; its humble dwellings have seen the comings and goings of generation upon generation of life's unfortunates, those with aspirations far above their origins and those whom this great city, Manchester, has drawn towards it like a magnet with the promise of better times to come.

From the Industrial Revolution to the Great Depression and onward into the 21st Century, the thoroughfare of Cheetham Hill Road has carried the ever-changing traffic of commerce and humanity issuing from the city.

The York Mail Coach has been replaced by the dedicated bus lane, cinemas have given way to shopping centres and religious buildings have altered in shape but Cheetham Hill Road is still the artery of north Manchester, as it has been for well over 400 years.

DEFINING CHEETHAM HILL

In writing this book the main focus has been on the thoroughfare of Cheetham Hill Road itself. However, it is impossible to ignore important and interesting aspects of some of the surrounding streets and districts. To do so would be rather like painting a portrait of a great person without showing their head.

There is, inevitably, a certain amount of duplication of information previously presented in 'A Crumpsall History', notably in the area where the border of Crumpsall coincides with Cheetham Hill Road, between the Half Way House and Greenhill Road.

The content mainly covers the period from 1800 to the mid-late 20th century.

Martin Gittins, 10th February 2021

York Street

A WORD FROM FRIEDRICH ENGELS:

> 'The villas of the upper classes, surrounded by gardens, lie in the higher and remoter parts of Chorlton and Ardwick or on the breezy heights of Cheetham Hill, Broughton and Pendleton.
>
> The upper classes enjoy healthy country air and live in luxurious and comfortable dwellings which are linked to the centre of Manchester by omnibuses which run every fifteen or thirty minutes.
>
> To such an extent has the convenience of the rich been considered in the planning of Manchester that these plutocrats can travel from their houses to their places of business in the centre of the town by the shortest routes, which run entirely through working-class districts, without even realising how close they are to the misery and filth which lie on both sides of the road.'

MONTY DOBKIN WRITING IN 'BROUGHTON AND CHEETHAM HILL IN REGENCY AND VICTORIAN TIMES':

> 'For quite some time Cheetham Hill was comparatively little affected by the Industrial Revolution, as the area had been chosen by the Manchester merchants for their country homes. They joined the landed gentry by purchasing large estates and building spacious mansions in private parks, yet they were within driving distance of their warehouses and factories.
>
> Cheetham Hill lacked many of the facilities which had attracted the first factories and so it was kept relatively free of industry and of other great changes, preserving the rural aspects which the merchants and landowners wanted for their own enjoyment. Thus, the early character of these districts as residential suburbs was established.
>
> The 70,000 people of Manchester were crowded into a very small area of today's inner city. A very short distance away the picture was very different. In great open spaces to the north of the town were several long-established, scattered settlements, the oldest of which was close to Prestwich Parish Church.
>
> There were groups of cottages in Rooden, near what is today Whittaker Lane, at Rainsough, The Cliff, Cheetham Hill, Smedley Lane and Cheetwood, and these were the main populated areas. The stately homes in their many acres of gardens and grounds occupied much of the rest of the landscape.'

EXTRACT FROM AN ARTICLE IN THE MANCHESTER EVENING NEWS IN 1970:

> "Not so long ago, Cheetham meant a steep climb through a warren of sooty brick where the greybeards sat wagging on the doorstep. A Lowry nightmare country of monstrous black churches and yawning graveyards. It has been part of the city now since 1838 and if you buy a raincoat the chances are it was made in one of these dingy little factories that used to be Methodist churches. Yet before that it was open country, dotted with hard bitten farms and cottages. You can still find little back streets, overlooked in the avalanche of slum clearance, where ginger cats dote on sooty windowsills and pallid sunflowers droop in the remains of cottage gardens

York Street

ACKNOWLDEGEMENTS

Wherever possible all content has been cross-checked for accuracy. Inevitably, when using information from sites such as Wikipedia there is an inherent risk that some details may be inaccurate.

I am indebted to the Facebook contributors, too numerous to name individually who, through their comments on pages such as 'I remember The Old Crumpsall', 'Did You Live in Cheetham or Cheetham Hill' and 'Cheetham and Crumpsall Heritage Society', have enabled me to tie up many loose ends and to fill gaps in my own research. We are truly fortunate to have the world at our fingertips in such a way.

I have not, knowingly, infringed anybody's copyright. All Illustrations used in the book come from either private sources, with permission, or from internet sources where no copyright information has been attached.

Thanks are due to anyone who has bought a copy of my first large-format book 'A Crumpsall History' or any of the Local History Books in the 'Bedford Falls Publications' list, and to those people who have joined me on any of the walks 'From The Green' or attended any talks I have given on Local History topics or who have come forward with their own stories which I have been able to turn into books.

Your continued interest makes it easier to continue with the writing process, even when it comes down to the tedious jobs of double-checking sources, re-reading and re-drafting sections and generally tidying up all the content.

Special thanks once again to the ever-patient and meticulous Irene Gittins for her assistance with proof-reading and formatting, and to Michael Perduniak for his valuable overview and analysis.

DEDICATION

This book is dedicated to my father, John Gittins, who was born on Cheetham Hill Road and raised in Temple Square and to my paternal grandparents, Charles and Annie Gittins.

York Street

CHAPTER I - ROMAN TIMES

What did Manchester look like before the encroachment of the city began its inexorable progress before, in fact, a city existed at all?

Even as far back as Roman times, this area had seen settlement and it is to this era that we must first turn.

It is likely that, prior to the arrival of Agricola in the first century A.D., there had existed a fortification occupied by the 'blue-shielded Brigantes' referred to by Agricola's son-in-law, the historian Tacitus. J. Tait, in his book 'Medieval Manchester and the Beginnings of Lancashire', tells us that the so-called fort at this site had:

> *'a rampart of earth and timber and the internal buildings were also timber.'*

This stood at the confluence of the Rivers Irk and Irwell, later known as Hunt's Bank, which was later to be the site of Chetham's College.

As an important defensive point at this river crossing, it controlled the road northwards which, in due course, became known as York Street, and eventually, Cheetham Hill Road.

Some fifty years later, when Emperor Hadrian abandoned the far north and built his historic wall, the main route from the south to the wall lay east of the Pennines, and passed close by what is now Catterick.

A major cross-country road ran between York and Chester and, as this passed though Lancashire, it was itself crossed by first a road from Warrington to Lancaster and then by one from Manchester to Ribchester, where there was a garrison of 1000 cavalry. Thus, Manchester became a vital point in the road network and, as such, warranted a larger, more fortified, encampment. This was built on a mound in a bend in the river Medlock at a place now known as Castlefield.

One possible origin of the name Manchester comes from this breast-shaped hill, hence 'Mamucium'.

We can imagine, then, the sound of Roman soldiers marching along the road from Manchester on their way northwards to Lancaster, Ribchester or York.

This does not explain, however, why Cheetham Hill Road was originally designated York Street, when such a name would have been more suitably given to Oldham Road, there being a section of 'Roman Road' at Failsworth and a Roman Fort at Castleshaw, north east of Oldham itself.

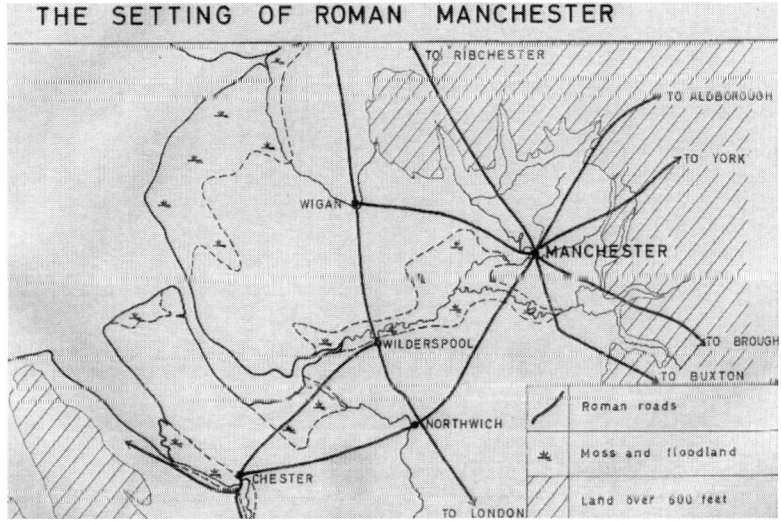

1

York Street

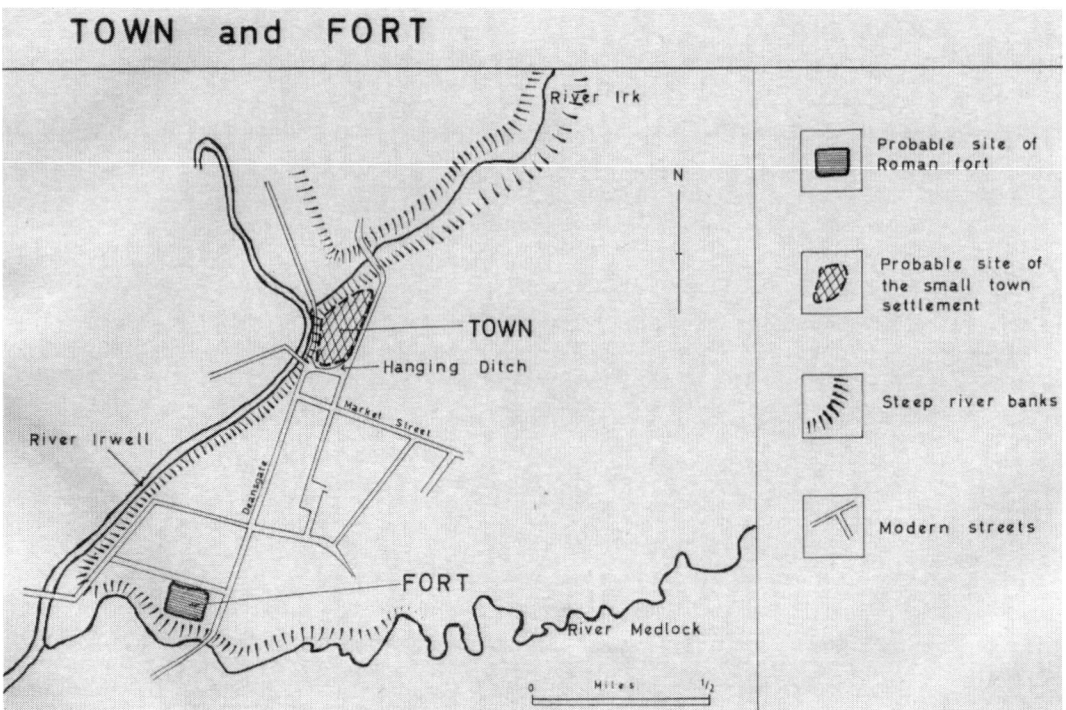

MAPS TAKEN FROM 'RICH INHERITANCE' BY N. FRANGOPULO

The original fortification of the Brigantes referred to by Tait would have been in the vicinity of the "small town settlement" indicated above. The route which crosses the River Irk just north of the town leads to Red Bank, whilst the route to the north-west becomes Great Cheetham Street. At this time York Street/Cheetham Hill Road did not exist. Red Bank wound its way northwards, becoming North Street and, when the main road was laid, the two routes would eventually meet where Stocks House stood, forming the junction of York Street and Dirty Lane (now Elizabeth Street).

THE CASE FOR TEMPLE.

Further north at Smedley Lane there was, from time immemorial, a group of houses collectively known as 'The Temple', or simply 'Temple'. This included an ancient bowling green by the same name, thought to have dated from Medieval times and later a public house, (which replaced the much earlier Eagle and Child) a cinema and a Primary School. On the opposite side of the road to the pub, from the early 19th century stood a grand villa called Temple House, with extensive grounds and even a lake. At the corner of Alms Hill Road stood Temple Bar, a toll bar controlling traffic.

Why should this name have been used in this place for so long, and what was the significance of it originally?

The author has pondered long and hard over this question and has a theory to propose. Perhaps it will be up to someone else to prove or discount it. Here, briefly, are the reasons for thinking that Temple has a strong Roman foundation.

1. Romans leaving a settlement and heading off to another (e.g., Manchester to Ribchester) would often pause early on the journey to make an offering at a wayside Temple.

2. Temples were often dedicated to Water Gods. There is evidence of many water courses and springs in Cheetham/Crumpsall (e.g., Springfield, Brookfield, Wellfield, Fountain Street, etc.) The author has heard a first-hand account of a water course culverted under houses on Smedley Lane. There are indications on early maps of 'risings' and 'sinks' in the area close to Smedley Lane.

York Street

3. Temple House[1] c.1830 stood on Cheetham Hill Road opposite St. Luke's church. It was on the corner of Bignor Street. Bignor Roman Villa is a large Roman courtyard villa which has been excavated and put on public display on the Bignor estate in the English county of West Sussex. It is well known for its high quality mosaic floors, which are some of the most complete and intricate in the country.

4. A pencil sketch was made in 1824 of a Roman altar which, at that time, was in the possession of M. Ainsworth of Smedley Lane.[2] It is clear that the altar was discovered elsewhere, but it may be that it was brought to Smedley Lane to be displayed there possibly because of the site's Roman connections.

THE AREA KNOWN AS 'TEMPLE' OR 'THE TEMPLE' WITH TEMPLE HOUSE OPPOSITE

---

[1] Temple House was, for many years, the property of Philip Lucas a cotton merchant and city councillor for Cheetham between 1851 and 1854. By the 1870s it was a school for young ladies

[2] Possibly the brother of William Harrison Ainsworth the novelist. When the boys were growing up, the family lived at Beech Hill, a grand residence on Smedley Lane, which may have remained in the family

York Street

Granted, there is only circumstantial evidence to support such a theory, but the author believes that there are strong indications of the likelihood of a Temple on the site. The ground where the bowling green was, has lain undisturbed since AT LEAST the middle of the 16th century and it is hoped that a geophysical survey of the area can be made at some time in the future to see if any evidence can be unearthed there.

It is worth noting that there is another public house called the Temple, in Sale, alongside Chester Road, another main Roman road. Perhaps there is a similar connection to be found there?

In the meantime, further research might reveal information in connection with both these areas.

From Roman times until the early years of the nineteenth century there is little written evidence of anything in connection with the area of Cheetham Hill Road. Court Leet Records tell of a few isolated incidents, mainly concerning disputes over land ownership, but it is not until the dawn of the Industrial Age that Cheetham Hill Road begins to flourish.

York Street

CHAPTER II - A LEISURELY STROLL

In this chapter we will take a metaphorical walk along Cheetham Hill Road, to set the scene for what is to follow and to acquaint the reader with the geography of the subject. By doing this, it is possible to relate the scenes described below with the present appearance of the thoroughfare in the 21st century, before delving further back to its earliest origins.

The texts are taken from two sources. The first and third descriptions are from the writings of T. Swindells and describe the scene around 1828 and 1848. The middle description comes from an article printed in 1961 in the Manchester Free Gazette. Sadly, the author is not identified, but the description gives a charming account of the road in 1839. These three accounts neatly illustrate the rapid pace of change that took place, even within the short space of 20 years.

Swindells 1828	Unknown Author 1839	Swindells 1848
Swindells' first description does not start in Manchester.  **ARCHIBALD PRENTICE**  **ABSALOM WATKIN**	From the church we pass Hunt's Bank to cross the River Irk where it joins the Irwell, by way of the bridge that leads to Strangeways. After crossing the Irk we see Moreton Street on our left hand side, there at No 27 lives Mr. Archibald Prentice, Printer and Publisher, who is a prominent Manchester Citizen of the day, having associations with well-known personages such as Absalom Watkins and Charles Dickens. 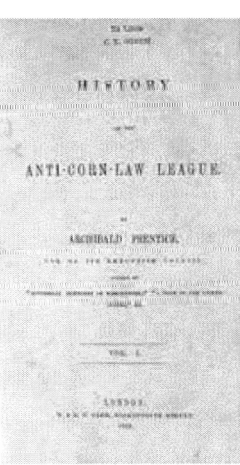 We proceed for about 200 yards and then turn sharp right up a rough track called Workhouse Brow, which rises fairly steeply for about 250 yards. The Workhouse itself is reached on the right.	Before another twenty years had passed away very great changes had taken place in Cheetham Hill and the road leading to it. From the corner of New Bridge Street to Stocks it was known as York Street, the name Cheetham Hill Road being limited to the length of roadway from there to the village. In describing the thoroughfare as it appeared sixty years ago it should be noticed at first that the toll bar which had stood at Ducie Bridge was removed in 1830. A few houses at the corner of Derby Street, and York Place on the left formed the only breaks in the fields that extended to Stocks House.  **SCOTLAND BRIDGE**

York Street

Just to the right, along the river, we can see Long Millgate, where it passes Mr. Howarth's house into Gibraltar and then crosses Miller's Lane till it reaches Ashley Lane at Scotland Bridge, leading to Red Bank.

THE STABLES AT STOCKS HOUSE

Stocks House is very pleasantly situated in its own grounds adjoining the Peel Estate down North Street.

Mr. Gilbert Winter then took up residence, becoming Borough Reeve in 1822, and director of the Liverpool and Manchester Railway. He was present at the opening of the first railway station in the world at the bottom of Priestnor Street (afterwards called Liverpool Road). The Duke of Wellington also officiated at the opening.

Stocks House, pleasantly situated, had not then lost its attractiveness, and on the opposite side of our thoroughfare was a farmer's lane known by the impressive name of Dirty Lane, now represented by Elizabeth Street.

Persons out late at night would, if alone, wait at the corner of the workhouse for the watchman coming on his down beat, and he would accompany them along the road.

On one particular night a confiding lady had entrusted herself to the care and keeping of the apparitors.

All went well until Halliwell Lane was reached where overhanging trees on either side of the road made the spot a favourable one for the perpetration of highway robbery and murder.

Whether the guide was suffering from an attack of nervous depression deponent sayeth not.

This terrace was only built three years ago, and must surely be one of the nicest terraces for many miles around. What a splendid uninterrupted view of the countryside from the second-floor windows.

These are not residences of the ordinary working man, and some well-known figures in Manchester life have taken residence here.

WILTON TERRACE

No more houses are reached until we reach Temple Cottage, where Samuel Schuster lives. Next to this is the 'Eagle and Child' tavern, Mary Burns being the landlady.

This is a fine old black and white frame house with projecting gables and is about 300 years old.

Beyond Wilton Terrace there were very few houses, the land on either side of the road being devoted to agricultural purposes.

The Temple, and the Bowling Green connected therewith, together with St. Luke's Church formed an interesting group.

York Street

But just as they were passing under the trees he said to the lady:

"Miss ____, it's very dark, aren't you feared?"

"No, Harry," replied the dauntless spinster.

"Well, I am!" said Harry, and off he set with his lantern as fast as his legs could carry him, leaving the lady to find her way home as best she could

JOHN CHIPPENDALL

FELIX MENDELSSOHN

During all these years there has been a bowling green at the rear of the tavern, and it must surely rank as one of the oldest in the country.

Curiously enough it never took the name of the pub, but was always called the Temple Bowling Green.

We are now at St. Luke's Church. This is a very fine new church built in 1836 for the huge sum of £23,000, the architect being Mr. T.W. Atkinson. John Chippindall is the first minister, and is no doubt looking forward to preaching the gospel in this expanding district.

During the last 20 years the population of Cheetham Hill has nearly doubled and there is now a population of close on 5,000 people.

There is a very fine wrought iron oil lamp at the outside post of both the north and south main gates, and the railings round the church with a total length of about 500 yards are ranked among the best in this part of the country. It is the intention to build a day school later.

I afterwards learned that in 1847 the great Mendelssohn played the new organ which had been installed there.

Further along on the left we next come to Halliwell Lane, so named after Mr. Halliwell, who built a house called "Broomfield" near the bowling green behind The Griffin Inn.

Also resident in Halliwell Lane at a large house called "Stonewall," lived the Henshaw family.

ST. LUKE'S CHURCH

DEMOLITION OF ST. LUKE'S

York Street

On his death on March 4th. 1810, Mr. Thos. Henshaw left the huge sum of £40,000 to maintain an institution for the blind.

Mrs. Henshaw, his wife, died in 1836, their daughter had married the Ed. Lloyd previously referred to, and lived at "Greenhill."

THOMAS HENSHAW

Eighty years ago, the Bird in Hand was the last house in the village, no other building being seen until Sandy Lane, now Crescent Road, was reached, where several substantial residences stood.

The inn itself was one of the most picturesque in the neighbourhood, and when in recent times it was removed, one of the most interesting of local landmarks disappeared.

In front of the Bird in Hand were water troughs for horses and nearby were the stocks.

ROBIN HOOD HOTEL

At the corner of Middleton Road stood a toll bar which was known as White Smithy bar because of the whitewashed smithy that stood on the opposite corner of the road.

Bird in Hand on the right. Just in front of this well-known pub is the stocks where local wrongdoers are placed to ponder over the error of their ways.

We can now see the village of Cheetham Hill on our left clustered round St. Mark's Church, which was built about 1794, and is next in age to The Collegiate and St. Ann's.

St. Mark's' first minister was the Rev. C. W. Ethelston, who died in 1830. he lived at Falcon Villas in Halliwell Lane.

On our right after the Bird in Hand is Sandy Lane. Along here at the junction of Sandy Lane with Humphrey Street stood, for many centuries, Crumpsall Hall, the birthplace of Humphrey Chetham.

The old Hall was pulled down in 1825 but many of its memories linger on.

Much of the old rural area still remains however, the only buildings just here consisting of a large mansion type house on the right in Sandy Lane and two or three large houses on the main road.

Mr. John Pelter is the landlord of the "Robin Hood" inn and almost opposite, in Sandy Lane was Mr. Pilkington's bow and arrow shop.

After passing here there are no more houses until we reach the end of our ramble at White Smithy toll-house.

ST. MARK'S

CRUMPSALL OLD HALL

WHITE SMITHY

York Street

The traveller of the twenty first century will have to look long and hard to find any evidence of much of what has been described here. There are a few reminders in the form of buildings which have been adapted for different uses, the odd gate post of a grand residence[3] and, of course, some of the street names remain to tell their story, but we have to thank Mr. Swindells for putting on record, so vividly, the appearance of Cheetham Hill Road in times past, and for Mr. Lomax of the Manchester Free Gazette for reprinting the 1839 version.

---

[3] The gatepost of a house called Mansefield can still be seen just opposite Brideoak Street

CHAPTER III - SOME NOTABLE RESIDENTS AND VISITORS

From the beginning of the 1800s Cheetham Hill Road started to become the most fashionable suburb of Manchester.

The closeness of the area to the warehouses and banks of the city, coupled with its elevated position overlooking the valley of The River Irk, made it a highly desirable place to live. The grand villas and terraces which sprung up along its length were statements of wealth for all to see.

Only a few yards from the squalor and degradation of Scotland and Red Bank, and the supposedly improved living conditions provided by Newtown, the merchants and bankers lived in grandeur, surrounded by lawns, lakes and follies for their own distraction and for the amusement of their equally-wealthy visitors from areas such as Ardwick Green.

It should come as no surprise to find that the great and the good of English literature, science and commerce rubbed shoulders along Cheetham Hill Road, or that for decades some of the most celebrated names of recent times were born or lived there.[4]

THE GRANT BROTHERS

The Grant brothers, William and Daniel were originally from Scotland but moved to Lancashire to seek their fortune, which they did, successfully, in the manufacture of textiles. Described by many who met them as 'unforgettable characters' they were, eventually, to be immortalised by the novelist Charles Dickens, who had heard reports of their distinguished careers and generosity and who is said to have met them at a dinner party in Manchester in 1839.

His observant eye saw them as the perfect models for 2 famous characters, the very exemplary brothers Charles and Ned Cheeryble, in his novel, "Nicholas Nickleby." Perhaps the greatest tribute ever paid to them is to be found in Dickens' preface to that book:

> *'It may be right to say that there are 2 characters in this book which are drawn from life …. Those who take an interest in this tale will be glad to learn that the Brothers Cheeryble do live; that their liberal charity, their singleness of heart, noble nature and unbounded benevolence are no creatures of the author's brain, but are prompting every day some munificent and generous deed in that town of which they are the pride and honour. May, 1848.'*

This was referring to William and Daniel Grant – ever afterwards known as "The Cheeryble Grants.

---

[4] All Biographies are drawn from multiple online and written sources

An un-proofed copy of the contents was included in error.
This is a corrected version.

CHAPTER I - ROMAN TIMES – Page 1

Roman Manchester – Town and Fort – Temple – Bignor Roman Villa – Roman Altar

CHAPTER II - A LEISURELY STROLL – Page 5

Strangeways Park – Archibald Prentice – Gibraltar and Scotland – Wilton Terrace
Job's Stile Path Eagle and Child Tavern – Felix Mendelssohn – C. W. Ethelston
Crumpsall Hall - Pilkington's Bow and Arrow Shop

CHAPTER III – SOME NOTABLE RESIDENTS AND VISITORS – Page 10

The Grant Brothers – Jack Rosenthal – Howard Jacobsen – Frances Hodgson Burnett
Benny Rothman – James Rawson – Joseph Hyman – James Crossley

CHAPTER IV – HOUSES AND BUILDINGS OF DISTINCTION – Page 24

Cheetham Town Hall - Cheetham Assembly Rooms – Prestwich Union Offices – Synagogues
Manchester Union Workhouse – Free Library and Reading Room – Northern Hospital
Cheetham Baths Jewish Museum – Rosen Hallas – Ryecroft House – Stocks House – Temple Square
Queens Road Bus and Tram Depot – Crumpsall District Library – Joseph Holt's Brewery

CHAPTER V – SMEDLEY, THE FORGOTTEN SUBURB – Page 36

Beech Hill – Smedley Hill – Edward Chippindall – Stowell Manor – Smedley Bank
William Harrison Ainsworth – George Condy – John Rylands – Eustratio Ralli
Nathan Laski – Smedley House

CHAPTER VI – PLACES OF WORSHIP AND EDUCATION - Page 51

St. Mark's   St. Luke's – Temple School – St. Chad's – Notre Dame Convent – Victoria Wesleyan
Ducie Wesleyan St. Mary's Ukrainian Catholic Church – Cheetham Hill Wesleyan Methodist - Trinity United
Heath Street School – The Khizra Masjid – The North Manchester Jamia Mosque - Rosen Hallas School
Early Jewish Schools – King David School - Spanish and Portuguese Synagogue - Older Synagogues

CHAPTER VII – ENTERTAINMENT AND LEISURE – Page 67

The Griffin   The Temple – The Crumpsall – The George – The Half Way House – The Robin Hood
The Derby Brewery Arms – The Empress – The Pleasant – Ukrainian Clubs – The Polish Club
Premier Cinemas – Temperance Billiard Hall – The Temple Pictorium – The Odeon – The Globe
The Shakespeare – The Bijou – The Majestic Skating Rink – Finnigan's Dance Academy
The Ice Palace - Cheetham Wakes

CHAPTER VIII – MISCELLANY – Page 81

Cheetwood Urban Village - Car Showrooms – Police Station – Hotels
Books featuring Cheetham Hill – The Monkey Run

York Street

JACK ROSENTHAL — Playwright

Jack Rosenthal was born in Cheetham Hill, Manchester, into a Jewish family. After studying English Literature at Sheffield University, he carried out his National Service in the Royal Navy. He worked briefly in advertising before joining Granada Television. He earned his first television credit with Granada in 1961, assigned as a writer of episode 31 of Britain's longest-running soap opera, *Coronation Street*. He became a regular writer for the series and began writing for other series as well.

During the 1960s, he contributed material for various television comedy shows including the satirical *That Was The Week That Was*. At Granada Television, he wrote a spin-off series from *Coronation Street* for the character Leonard Swindley, played by Arthur Lowe, called *Pardon the Expression* and created two comedy series *The Dustbinmen* and *The Lovers* starring Richard Beckinsale and Paula Wilcox.

Rosenthal won three BAFTA awards for *Bar Mitzvah Boy* (about a Jewish boy's Bar Mitzvah), *The Evacuees* (based on his own war-time evacuation) and *Spend, Spend, Spend* (about the football pools winner, Viv Nicholson). He also wrote *The Knowledge,* a film about London taxi-drivers which has become a classic for cabbies-in-training. He created *London's Burning* as a one-off drama in 1986, and this later developed into a long-running TV drama.

In 1983, Rosenthal co-wrote the film *Yentl* with Barbra Streisand. He also did uncredited work on the screenplay of *Chicken Run*.

He married actress Maureen Lipman in 1974; they have two grown-up children, writers Amy Rosenthal and Adam Rosenthal. Jack Rosenthal was a Manchester United fan all his life.

Rosenthal was awarded the CBE in 1994. He died of cancer in Barnet, London, aged 72, on 29 May 2004. He is buried in Golder's Green Jewish Cemetery.

His autobiography, *By Jack Rosenthal* was published posthumously and a four-part adaptation by his daughter, titled *Jack Rosenthal's Last Act*, was broadcast to great acclaim on BBC Radio 4 in July 2006 starring Maureen Lipman as herself and Stephen Mangan as Jack Rosenthal.

RALPH BRIDEOAKE – Clergyman

Ralph Brideoake, was the son of Richard Brideoake of Cheetham Hill.

Born in 1612, and baptised on 31 January at the Collegiate Church, Manchester, Brideoake graduated from Brasenose College, Oxford with a B.A. in 1634, and was made an M.A. by Charles I of England in 1636.

Beginning in 1638, Brideoake was High Master at Manchester Free School, but lost the position because of his Royalist affiliation. He became chaplain to James Stanley, 7th Earl of Derby, a Royalist leader, and was besieged at Lathom House with Stanley's family in 1644.

He interceded, unsuccessfully, with William Lenthall, Speaker of Parliament, for a stay of the execution of the Earl. In 1651 Brideoake then became his chaplain.

Brideoake was Vicar of Witney from 1654. On the Restoration, he became Rector of Standish in 1660, Dean of Salisbury in 1667 and Bishop of Chichester in 1675.

York Street

In 1660 he was appointed Canon of the eleventh stall at St George's Chapel, Windsor Castle, a position he held until 1678. He died on 5 October 1678, and is buried in St. George's Chapel, Windsor Castle.

He is remembered in the naming of Brideoak Street, Cheetham.

JESSE FOTHERGILL – Novelist

Jesse Fothergill was born at Cheetham Hill in Manchester on 7 June 1851. During her relatively short career in the later nineteenth century, Jessie Fothergill produced fourteen novels, many of which ran to several editions, and which were serialised in Indian and Australian journals.

Although she is often classified as a regional writer, her fiction explores and depicts "a self-consciously modern world" where issues of class, religion, gender, sexuality and race are scrutinized and debated.

Her work was regularly compared by her contemporaries with that of Elizabeth Gaskell and George Eliot. It is now the subject of increased attention and re-evaluation.

In 1875 she published her first novel, *Healey, A Romance*, in three volumes. Her most popular and best-known work, *The First Violin*, was serialised anonymously in *Temple Bar*. After this it appeared in three volumes with her initials. Later editions carried her name.

On 28 July 1891 soon after her fortieth birthday, she died suddenly at Bern in Switzerland on her way home from Italy. Her last novel, *Oriole's Daughter*, was published in London in three volumes.

THOMAS HENSHAW – Manufacturer and Philanthropist

Thomas Henshaw, the founder of Henshaw's School for the Blind, died on March 4th. 1810, at Stonewall, a delightful old house that formerly stood opposite the end of Halliwell Lane.

Henshaw, who was of humble origin, was born at Prestbury in 1747. He settled in Oldham in 1775 and became very successful as a felt hat manufacturer. By his will he devised £20,000 each for the founding of a Blue Coat School in Oldham, and a Blind Asylum in Manchester.

In a later codicil he increased the amount for the former institution to £40,000. The money was left for the maintenance of the institutions named, the testator anticipating that the funds requisite for the purchase of sites and the erection of buildings would be contributed by others.

His will was contested by family members for 26 years, but was eventually upheld by the Court of Chancery in favour of the scheme.

A lawsuit ensued, but in the end, legacies were declared to be valid. In 1834 a public subscription was opened to provide the funds necessary for the erection of a blind asylum to which was added a deaf and dumb school. In September 1834 the Board of Management of Henshaw's Blind Asylum and Deaf and Dumb schools, jointly purchased a plot of land adjoining the botanical gardens at Old Trafford Manchester.

York Street

In 1837 Henshaw's Blind Asylum, later known as Henshaw's Institution for the Blind, was founded in a building built with public contributions in Old Trafford.

The foundation stone was laid on March 23rd. 1836 by William Grant, and the building was opened on June 21st. 1837, with a public procession. Mrs. Henshaw, widow of Thomas Henshaw, died at Stonewall on April 8th. 1836. Their daughter married Edward Loyd, the banker, who resided at Greenhill, a mansion that formerly stood on Cheetham Hill Road.

The house had been erected by Samuel Jones, the founder of the well-known banking concern, whose sister married the Rev. Lewis Loyd, the Unitarian minister who also became a partner in the banking business. Samuel Jones died at Greenhill in 1819 and the house was occupied by Edward Loyd for some years afterwards. Loyd was an owner of extensive property in the area, and evidence can be seen on the Tithe Map and registers.

J. J. THOMSON – Physicist

Joseph John Thomson who discovered the electron and won the Nobel Prize was born in Cheetham Hill on 18 December 1856, the eldest son of antiquarian book seller and publisher Joseph James and his wife Emma.

His early education was in small private schools where he demonstrated outstanding talent and an interest in science. In 1870 he was admitted to Owens College at the unusually young age of 14. His parents planned to enrol him as an apprentice engineer to Sharp-Stewart & Co, a locomotive manufacturer, but these plans were cut short when his father died in 1873.

He moved on to Trinity College, Cambridge in 1876. In 1880 he obtained his BA in mathematics. He applied for and became a Fellow of Trinity College in 1881. Thomson received his MA in 1883. Thomson was elected a Fellow of the Royal Society on 12 June 1884 and, in the same year, accepted the position of Cavendish Professor of Physics. He served as President of the Royal Society from 1915 to 1920.

He was awarded a Nobel Prize in 1906, "in recognition of the great merits of his theoretical and experimental investigations on the conduction of electricity by gases." He was knighted in 1908 and appointed to the Order of Merit in 1912.

In 1918 he became Master of Trinity College, Cambridge, where he remained until his death on 30 August 1940; his ashes rest in Westminster Abbey, near the graves of Sir Isaac Newton and his former student, Ernest Rutherford

HOWARD JACOBSEN — Author

Howard Jacobsen was born and raised in Cheetham, brought up in Prestwich, and educated at Stand Grammar School in Whitefield, before going on to study English at Downing College, Cambridge He lectured for three years at the University of Sydney before returning to Britain to teach at Selwyn College, Cambridge. His later teaching posts included a period at Wolverhampton Polytechnic from 1974 to 1980.

Jacobson has been married three times. He married his first wife Barbara in 1964, when he was 22, with whom he has one son, Conrad. He married his second wife, Rosalin Sadler, in 1978. They divorced in 1995. In 2005, Jacobson was married for the third time, to radio and TV documentary maker Jenny De Yong.

In August 2014, Jacobson was one of 200 public figures who were signatories to a letter to The Guardian urging Scots to vote no to independence in the run-up to September's Scottish independence referendum.

The time he spent at Wolverhampton Polytechnic was to form the basis of his first novel, *Coming from Behind,* a campus comedy about a failing polytechnic that plans to merge facilities with a local football club.

His fiction, particularly in the dozen or so novels he has published since 1998, is characterised chiefly by a discursive and humorous style. Recurring subjects in his work include male-female relations and the Jewish experience in Britain in the mid to late 20th century. He has been compared to prominent Jewish-American novelists such as Philip Roth. Jacobson described *Kalooki Nights* as:

'the most Jewish novel that has ever been written by anybody, anywhere.'

As well as writing fiction, he also contributes a weekly column for The Independent newspaper.[5] In recent times, he has, on several occasions, attacked anti-Israel boycotts, and for this reason has been labelled a Liberal Zionist.

In October 2010 Jacobson won the Man Booker Prize for his novel *The Finkler Question*, which explores what it means to be Jewish today and is also about love, loss and male friendship.

DON ARDERN – Music Agent and Manager

Born Harry Levy, Don Ardern achieved notoriety in England for his aggressive, sometimes illegal business tactics which led to him being called 'Mr. Big', 'The English Godfather' and 'The Al Capone of Pop.'

He was the father of Sharon Osbourne (father-in-law of Ozzy Osbourne) and David Levy, by his wife, Hope Shaw, a former ballet dancer/teacher, who predeceased him, dying in 1998.

Born in Cheetham Hill, Arden began his show business career, when he was just 13 years old, as a singer and stand-up comic after briefly attending the Royal College of Music and, in 1944, changed his name from Harry Levy to Don Arden.

After the war Arden worked as an entertainer on the British variety circuit. He impersonated famous tenors, like Enrico Caruso, and movie gangsters such as Edward G. Robinson and George Raft. On weekends, Yiddish-speaking Arden impressed Jewish audiences with his Al Jolson routine.

He gave up performing in 1954 to become a showbiz agent, after realising it would be more profitable. He began his career organising Hebrew folk song contests. Arden signed up American rock 'n' roller Gene Vincent in 1960, thus launching his career as a manager.

After several years of bringing American performers including Bo Diddley and Chuck Berry to tour Britain, Arden became Vincent's manager. For a short period of time in the early 1960s he managed up-and-coming Salford singer Elkie Brooks, who went on to become a household name some years later.

---

[5] Correct at the time of writing

York Street

In 1965, Arden met aspiring rock band Small Faces in his office in Carnaby Street. Half an hour later he had signed them up. In 1967, however, Arden sold the Small Faces' contract to Andrew Oldham, the former manager of The Rolling Stones. Oldham paid Arden £25,000 in cash and delivered it, at his request, in a brown paper bag.

In 1968 he signed The Move, and struck gold when he added two groups, ELO and Wizzard. In 1973 Arden took over management of singer-songwriter Lynsey De Paul.

In 1979, one of Arden's successes, Black Sabbath, sacked their vocalist Ozzy Osbourne. Arden's daughter Sharon began to date Osbourne, and took over his management from her father. Arden was livid. Reportedly, the next time Sharon visited Don, his vicious pet dogs savaged her. She was pregnant, and lost the child.

Sharon eventually married Osbourne and had no contact with her father for 20 years. In 2001 she told The Guardian newspaper:

"The best lesson I ever had was watching him mess his business up. He taught me everything not to do. My father's never even seen any of my three kids and, as far as I'm concerned, he never will."

Later the same year, under Ozzy's insistence, Sharon and Arden finally reconciled, with Arden making a walk-on role in the successful reality TV show The Osbournes in 2002. He also met his grandchildren Jack and Kelly for the first time.

From 1986 to the mid-1990s, Arden shuttled between his homes in Beverly Hills and Parkside, in Wimbledon, London. In August 2004 Sharon Osbourne stated her father had Alzheimer's disease. A 'Tell all' biography about Arden's life, entitled 'Mr. Big', was published in 2007. Sharon Osbourne paid for her father's care in the last years of his life. On 29 October 2007, a memorial headstone was unveiled at Agecroft Jewish Cemetery Manchester. A line of inscription on the stone reads:

'His beautiful voice will sing in our hearts forever. Shalom.'

FRANCES HODGSON BURNETT – Author

Frances Eliza Hodgson was born in 1849 at 141 York Street in Cheetham.

She was the third of five children, with two older brothers and two younger sisters. Their parents were Edwin Hodgson, an ironmonger from Doncaster in Yorkshire, and his wife Eliza Boond, from a well-to-do Manchester family. Hodgson owned a business in Deansgate, selling quality ironmongery and brass goods. The family lived comfortably, employing a maid and a nurse-maid.

In 1852 the family moved about a mile further along York Street to a more spacious home in a newly-built terrace, opposite St Luke's Church, with greater access to outdoor space.

Barely a year later, Hodgson died of a stroke, leaving the family without income. Frances was cared for by her grandmother while her mother took over running the family business.

From her grandmother, who bought books for her, Frances learned to love reading, in particular *The Flower Book*, which had coloured illustrations and poems.

Because of their reduced income, Eliza had to give up their house and moved with her children to Seedley Grove, Tanners Lane, Pendleton, Salford. There they lived, with relatives, in a home that included a large enclosed garden, in which Frances enjoyed playing.

York Street

When her mother moved the family to Islington Square, Salford, Frances mourned the lack of flowers and gardens. Their home was located in a gated square of faded gentility, adjacent to an area with severe overcrowding and poverty, that "defied description", according to Friedrich Engels, who lived in Manchester at the time.

In 1863, Eliza Hodgson was forced to sell their business and move the family once again to an even smaller home. At that time Frances' limited education came to an end. Eliza's brother, William Boond, asked the family to join him in Knoxville, Tennessee. Within the year Eliza decided to accept his offer and move the family from Manchester. She sold their possessions and told Frances to burn her early writings in the fire. In 1865, the family emigrated to the United States and settled near Knoxville.

In 1872 Frances married Swan Burnett, a medical doctor. Burnett then began to write novels, the first of which *That Lass o' Lowrie's*, was published to good reviews. *Little Lord Fauntleroy* was published in 1886 and made her a popular writer of children's fiction, although her romantic adult novels were also popular.

Burnett enjoyed socializing and lived a lavish lifestyle. Beginning in the 1880s, she began to travel to England frequently and in the 1890s bought a house, where she wrote *The Secret Garden*. Her oldest son, Lionel, died of tuberculosis in 1890, which caused a relapse of the depression she had struggled with for much of her life. She divorced Swan Burnett in 1898, married Stephen Townsend in 1900, and divorced him in 1902. A few years later she settled in Nassau County, Long Island, where she died in 1924 and is buried in Roslyn Cemetery.

BENNY ROTHMAN – Political Activist

Bernard Rothman, better known as Benny Rothman, (June 1, 1911 - January 23, 2002) was most famous for his leading role in the Mass Trespass of Kinder Scout in 1932.

Born in Cheetham Hill, Manchester, to a Jewish family, Rothman's poor family circumstances dictated that he start work at the earliest opportunity, rather than take full advantage of a scholarship that he had won.

Working as an errand boy in the motor trade, he studied geography and economics in his spare time while his Aunt Ettie introduced him to *The Ragged-Trousered Philanthropists* and the works of Upton Sinclair.

Increasingly committed to the causes of socialism and communism, Rothman lost his job after getting into some trouble with the law while selling copies of the Daily Worker. During a period of unemployment, with the help of a bicycle salvaged from spare parts, he discovered the nearby wilderness regions of the Peak District and North Wales.

The combination of his political activism and interest in the outdoors led to his participation in the Mass Trespass of 1932, an enterprise that resulted in a spell in prison and further employment difficulties.

In 1934, Rothman went to work at Avro (A.V. Roe) in Newton Heath and instantly became an officer of the Amalgamated Engineering Union (A.E.U.). At Avro's he met and married fellow communist Lily Crabtree but his political views became increasingly visible to his employer and he was dismissed. Rothman was active in working with Jewish groups in Manchester to oppose the campaigns of Sir Oswald Mosley's British Union of Fascists. In 1936, he started work at Metropolitan Vickers at Trafford Park and was again soon an A.E.U. official. Until his death from a stroke, he was active in a wide range of political and conservation movement campaigns and organisations.

York Street

JAMES RAWSON – Archer

World-class archer James Rawson, who reputedly never lost a match in his long successful career, is buried in the churchyard of the former St. Mark's Church in Cheetham Hill.

> 'St. Mark's Church, of which nothing now remains, was built in 1794 on what was the training ground of Rawson's sporting club, the Cheetham Hill Archers.
>
> Archery groups were popular in north Manchester in the eighteenth century, with Thomas Egerton, of Heaton Hall, being a prime member of rival group the Middleton Archers.
>
> These clubs have made their mark in modern times on local pubs such as the Robin Hood on Cheetham Hill Road, which was known as the Shooting Butt Inn back when the archers themselves would have been regulars. The Middleton Archer, on Kemp Street, in Middleton also owes its name to the sporting heritage of the area.'[6]

T. Swindells gives this detailed account of James' life and exploits:

> 'More than a century ago (c1800) the village of Cheetham Hill was noted for the skill of certain of its natives in archery. Pilkington's bow and arrow shop and Hyde's smithy at Sandy Lane, where an arrow could be tipped for a penny, were popular institutions.
>
> James Rawson was a handloom weaver and lived most of his life in an old house, now in ruins, opposite the Griffin Inn. Weavers were then well off and could afford to indulge in many amusements. Archery was then a favourite amusement, not only with the rich but with tradesmen and working people also.
>
> James appears to have begun shooting early, and even in boyhood to have acquired extraordinary proficiency, so that, as his gravestone has it, "from the age of 16 to 60 he never refused a challenge nor ever lost a match."
>
> When he became too old to weave, the gentlemen employed him to attend on shooting days and keep their bows in order, and when they had a friendly match with other villages they would dress him up as a gentleman to take part with them so as to get the benefit of his score; and it is said that at one of these matches held at Prestwich, the affair was so well contested that James and his opponent, the last two were on equal terms, and the last two arrows had to decide the match.
>
> When the Prestwich player sent his arrow the game appeared settled, as it had struck within an inch of the centre of the target, and the shaft lay a little obliquely, so as to cross the centre.
>
> But James sent his arrow with such truth and force that it split the other one and struck the very place required. This was considered to be the greatest feat in archery since the time of Robin Hood.
>
> When he died the gentlemen archers attended the funeral, and paid all expenses, including that of a gravestone.'

---

[6] Extract from 'Played in Manchester' by James Inglis

Rawson is buried in St. Mark's Churchyard, where his gravestone bears the following epitaph:

Here were interred the earthly remains of

JAMES RAWSON,

Who died October 1st, 1795; aged 80 years

His dexterity as an archer was unrivalled; from the age of

16 to 60 he never refused a challenge, nor lost a match.

Grim death grown jealous of his art,

His matchless fame to stop,

Relentless aimed th' unerring dart

And split the vital prop.

This favourite son Apollo eyed,

His virtues to requite,

Conveyed his spirit to reside

In realms of endless light.

**ST MARK'S CHURCH[7] (NOW DEMOLISHED) WHERE JAMES RAWSON IS BURIED.
HIS WAS ONE OF THE FIRST INTERMENTS IN THE CHURCHYARD,
THE CHURCH ONLY HAVING BEEN ESTABLISHED THE YEAR BEFORE HIS DEATH.**

JOSEPH ABRAHAM HYMAN - Survivor of the Titanic Liner Disaster

Mr. Joseph Abraham Hyman (pictured here with his wife) was born within the Russian Empire on 15 February 1881. He came to England as a young man and settled within Manchester's thriving Jewish community. He was married in 1902 to Esther Levy and they lived at 45 Stocks Street, Cheetham, Manchester, he was described as a storekeeper.

---

[7] See Chapter 6 for further details about the church

York Street

Abraham boarded the *Titanic* in Southampton as a third-class passenger and he was travelling alone to Springfield, Massachusetts, where he had a brother, Harry. He was listed as a picture frame maker.

He later described his escape:

"...The forward deck was jammed with the people, all of them pushing and clawing and fighting, and so I walked forward and stepped over the end of the boat that was being got ready and sat down."

He told The New York Times. *"Nobody disturbed me, and then a line of men gathered along the side and only opened when a woman or a child came forward. When a man tried to get through, he would be pushed back..."*

Reaching America aboard S.S. **Carpathia**, Abraham was met by his brother and granted several interviews to local newspapers. His wife refused to cross the Atlantic to join him and Abraham also had reservations about making the crossing again.

While Joseph was in America, he saw a type of shop that had not been seen in England and when he arrived back, he started a small delicatessen, modelled on what he saw, called J.A. Hyman Ltd.

Word of his amazing escape spread and he became a local celebrity where people would point and say "Look it's the man from the Titanic". It didn't take long for the shop to be known as "Titanics" a name that stuck with most of its customers.

The shop, originally on Cheetham Hill Road, adopted the name 'Titanics' and thrived for just over a century. In November 2016 Manchester's oldest kosher delicatessen was itself sunk, a victim of increased competition and diminished customer loyalty.

Joseph Hyman spent his later years living at 25 Crumpsall lane, Crumpsall. He died on 6 March 1956 in The Victoria Memorial Jewish Hospital in Manchester. He is buried in North Manchester Blackley Jewish cemetery, Manchester, England (section G, plot 172).[8]

GEORGE AUGUSTUS LEE (1761–1826) Industrialist

He was managing partner in a mill in Salford known as Philips and Lee. Lee's character was described in an obituary:

"Mr. Lee became early imbued with a love of the sciences, and was afterwards remarkable for the extent and precision of his acquirements in them. He had a quick and almost intuitive perception of the advantages to be derived from applying to useful purposes the great inventions that distinguished the era in which he lived, and the rare faculty of directing them, with energy and perseverance, to the fulfilment of extensive and important designs."

Aware of the advantages of the steam-engine soon after the **improvements of James Watt,** Lee installed steam power for the cotton-spinning machinery. A new mill, was erected from 1799 to 1801: it was an iron-framed building, the second such building in Britain. He knew of the experiments in gas lighting by William Murdoch and, in 1805, gas lighting was introduced, the first for a cotton mill. There was steady improvement of the machinery. Steam was used for heating the building, and a sick scheme was organised for the workforce. The company survived the period of **the Napoleonic Wars.** The mill was regarded as a model enterprise; it was one of Manchester's sights, and industrialists and scientists visited it.[9]

---

[8] Encyclopedia-titanica.org

[9] https://en.wikipedia.org/wiki/Smedley,_Manchester

York Street

LOUIS CHARLES CASARTELLI – Fourth Bishop of Salford (R.C.)

Rev. Casartelli was born of Italian parents in Cheetham Hill on 14th November 1852. He was educated at Salford Grammar School, of which institution he was one of the first pupils – an institution which had been founded by Dr. Turner, the first Bishop of Salford (1851 to 1872).

From there he went to Ushaw College and studied for a degree of the London University, achieving an M.A. and carrying off the much-coveted Gold Medal for Classics. He then went to the University of Louvain, Belgium, where he studied Linguistics and Philological Studies and, in particular, Oriental Languages. Whilst at Louvain he was ordained priest.

In 1877 he was appointed a professor and Prefect of Studies at St Bede's College, Manchester and in 1891 he was appointed Rector of the same. He continued his studies into Oriental Literature, the Religious Philosophy of Zoroastrianism the sacred tongues of Brahmins and Parsees

He was a long-time member of the Manchester Geographical Society for whom he wrote the first book on Commercial Geography. He was president of the Manchester Statistical Society and a member of the Manchester Education Committee of the Manchester Chamber of Commerce.

On 28 August 1903 Louis was appointed Bishop of Salford where he served until his death in 1925.

JAMES CROSSLEY - Founder of The Chetham Society

> 'Known to many as 'Manchester's Dr Johnson', James Crossley was a writer, editor and significant literary presence in the city, as well as a prolific book-collector, amassing well over 100,000 volumes of which many were of antiquarian interest. He lived for some years at Stocks House, Cheetham Hill Road.
>
> James Crossley was born in Halifax in 1800, the second son of a wealthy wool merchant. He was educated at Hipperholme Grammar School, as well as through the contents of his father's own private library, developing an extensive knowledge of classical literature at an early age.
>
> At the age of sixteen, he came on a visit to Manchester and spent time at Chetham's Library, an experience which made a deep impression upon him and almost certainly influenced the path of his own life.
>
> He was the owner of a precocious writing talent, and at the age of nineteen was already contributing articles to magazines and journals such as the Retrospective Review.
>
> In 1817 Crossley began his legal career, becoming articled to Thomas Ainsworth, a Manchester solicitor. Here he struck up what was to become a lifelong friendship with Ainsworth's son William Harrison Ainsworth, who would himself become a well-known writer and author of nearly forty historical novels.
>
> Crossley continued to practice law until his retirement in 1860, as well as giving time to political work for the Conservative Party and indulging his literary and antiquarian interests. In 1843 he and a group of friends founded the Chetham Society, which held its first meeting at the Library. He undertook much of the publishing work himself, as well as writing and editing many of the early volumes.

York Street

As a literary figure, Crossley's influence and importance can hardly be overstated. He was on numerous committees, was President of the Athenaeum and was elected a Fellow of the Society of Antiquaries, as well as making extensive contributions to 'Notes and Queries'.

He never married, but was a well-known and recognisable figure on the Manchester literary circuit and a popular and knowledgeable public speaker. In the later years of his life, he was often to be seen making his way to Chetham's Library wearing his customary dark cloak and wide-brimmed hat over his long silver hair.

Crossley was an avid book collector throughout his life, amassing an enormous number of volumes which amounted to probably the largest private library in Manchester. After his move to Stocks House in Cheetham Hill in 1878, he continued to collect, making piles of books on any available surface including the floor and the staircase. Indeed, so many books were piled on the stairs that in his later years he was no longer able to reach the first floor of his house.

Despite Crossley's attachment to Chetham's, only a handful of his collection is to be found at the Library. His personal library was dispersed by auction after his death, and many of the treasures he collected were lost to the city.'[10]

JAMES HALLIWELL

Before James Halliwell came from his home town of Bury to live in Cheetham Hill in 1788, the road which now bears his name was merely a cart track, leading to some farmers' fields in the area around Tetlow Fold.

It was alongside this track that he built his house, Broomfield, which backed onto the Griffin bowling green.

Halliwell was no great scholar in reading but he displayed an aptitude for mathematics which served him well in business.

An amusing story is told of an unusual event which took place as a result of Halliwell's lack of reading:

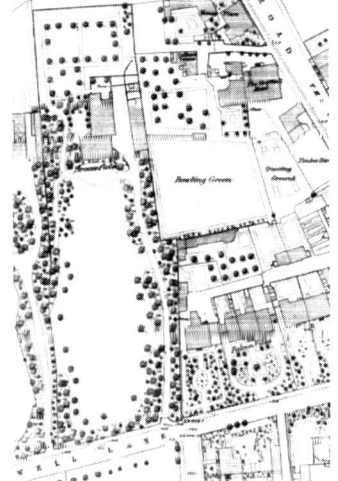

> *'On one occasion he sent a gift to a friend in London who, in acknowledging the receipt of it, said that he hoped "to send an equivalent shortly." The word equivalent was a new one to the unlettered businessman, who made it out to mean elephant.*
>
> *He accordingly had a high wall built round a small field behind his house and was preparing to build a suitable house, when a friend, seeing the preparations, asked the purport of them.*
>
> *A few words sufficed to show Mr. Halliwell how thoroughly he had misunderstood his correspondent's letter, and both friends had a hearty laugh about it.'*[11]

---

[10] Extract from the Chetham's Library website

[11] Manchester Streets and Manchester Men, T. Swindells

York Street

GEORGE WILSON

Originally from Hathersage in Derbyshire, George came to Manchester with his family and went into business as a starch manufacturer, residing at Moreton Street, on the opposite side of Cheetham Hill Road to Stocks House. He was briefly a Manchester Councillor in the St. Michael's Ward but turned his attention to the Reform Bill of 1832.

A proposal for the incorporation of Manchester around this time was met with strong opposition. However, Wilson, along with Richard Cobden and others were strongly in favour and, owing to his organisational skills the object was achieved relatively easily.

For seven years he was the chairman of The Anti-Corn Law League – Cobden described him as a "born chairman".

In other areas he was a true innovator. In 1847, telegraph wires were being laid between Manchester and Leeds. Richard Cobden was standing for Parliament for West Yorkshire and Wilson, who was a director of the Electric Telegraph Company, had miles of cable laid temporarily to Wakefield and was then able to telegraph the news of the election directly to Manchester. At two o'clock on the day of the election a report appeared in The Manchester Times – the first ever telegraphic newspaper report.

He originated the Night Asylum – a place for homeless people to sleep - and his work in many other areas was respected and admired by the people of Manchester.

He died in 1870 and was buried in Ardwick Cemetery.

JOHN HARLAND

John Harland, born in Hull, came to Manchester in 1830 and lived on Brideoak Street.

He trained as a letterpress printer but soon developed the skill of shorthand, becoming one of the most expert writers in the country. He secured a position as a reporter with The Manchester Guardian. He travelled to courthouses around the county and it was often said that his report of a trial at Lancaster was printed in The Guardian before the judge and jury had recovered from their exertions of the day.

Harland became known as the Father of Provincial Reporting. The Guardian gradually moved from weekly to daily publication and at the same time, Harland rose from reporter to editor.

In addition to his reporting and editorial work he was an expert in antiquarian manuscripts and inscriptions and an active member of The Chetham Society, for which he compiled and edited over a dozen volumes, including the Court Leet Records, *Mamecestre* and *The History of the Barony*.

Perhaps his most enduring work, however, still referenced today by folk historians, was the volume wrote with T.T. Wilkinson *Lancashire Folk-Lore*.

He was revising Edward Baines's *Lancashire* at the time of his death 1868.

York Street

E. W. BINNEY

E.W. Binney came to Manchester in 1836 at the age of 24 and lived in the house which was to be the home of John Harland some time later.

He founded the Manchester Geological Society and was an active member of the Literary and Philosophical Society, becoming its chairman, a post held from 1842 until his death in 1881.

On the Coal Measures in the Manchester area, in particular, he became an acknowledged authority.

He was elected a fellow of the Geological Society in 1853 and The Royal Society in 1856. He died at Cheetham Hill in 1881 and was interred at Worsley.

JOHN BROOKS

John Brooks was born in Whalley in 1786.

He became a successful businessman and was a partner in the banking firm of Grimshaw and Brooks. He was an early and very vocal proponent of The Anti-Corn Law League and worked tirelessly for the cause until his health failed.

He died at his home, Clarendon House, Crumpsall in 1849.

He was remembered as a man who was exceedingly tolerant of others, regardless of their political views, and a benevolent and generous master to those who worked for him.

ROBERT NEILL

Councillor for the Cheetham Ward, Neill was twice Lord Mayor of the city, serving consecutive terms in 1866-7 and 1867-68.

During his second term of office, he laid the foundation stones of both the Police Courts, Minshull Street, and the new Town Hall in Albert Square.

York Street

CHAPTER IV - HOUSES AND BUILDINGS OF DISTINCTION

The area to the north of the city, particularly the immediate vicinity of Cheetham Hill Road has some of the finest examples of the Victorian Villa style of building. Many of these were in the form of large, imposing terraces of houses but, by far the most impressive, were detached or semi-detached dwellings of considerable stature.

The boom of Manchester as a centre for the distribution of cotton goods led to the building of many substantial warehouses in the city centre, in areas such as Piccadilly, Portland Street and Whitworth Street. Buildings on a scale previously unseen transformed the shape and size of the 'mere village' of Manchester and established it as truly the first industrial city in the world.

These 'Cotton Canyons' stood as proud testament to the entrepreneurial spirit of the age and to the conviction of the cotton barons whose investment had made them possible.

It was only fitting, therefore, that these same cotton barons should want to display their wealth and power to the world at large and they did so in the way that people of power have done since time immemorial - they built big houses.

If the skyscraper penthouse is the status-symbol of the 21st century celebrity, then the 'big house' with its fancy gardens, staff of servants and imposing features was the badge of the early industrial magnates.

Naturally, the 'man of property' would have a checklist to consider when deciding just where to build his pile. It must be close to the centre of business but far enough away from the stink of poverty.

It must be visible, but unattainable to those of a lower status, and, above all, it must be in the most desirable location that the latest trend dictated.

The boundary separating Manchester from the district of Cheetham crossed Cheetham Hill Road at Knowsley Street. The faded remains of a boundary marker can still be seen on the side of the Derby Brewery Arms.

By the middle of the nineteenth century, Cheetham Hill and Smedley were rapidly becoming some of Manchester's wealthiest suburbs. It was here that the first of the civic buildings outside the town centre started to rise.

CHEETHAM HILL TOWN HALL

> 'Built between 1853 and 1855 in a restrained, Italianate Palazzo style of brick, with stone dressings, it comprised a main block of seven bays, with a three-bay projecting centre and two side wings set back, with an elegant iron and glass porte-cochere protecting the main entrance door.
>
> The foundation stone was laid in 1854 and the official opening took place in January 1855'[12]

The building remains although now it is an Indian buffet restaurant and event venue.

---

[12] Taken from The Builder Magazine

York Street

THE CHEETHAM ASSEMBLY ROOMS

'The Cheetham Assembly Rooms were amongst the most elaborate, elegant and beautiful chambers in the North of England. They were designed by Manchester architects Mills and Murgatroyd and erected in the 1850s with interior decoration from John Gregory Crace.

There had been other assembly rooms in Manchester in St. Ann's Street and in Mosley Street. When the latter closed, money was eventually found to build again, this time in the prosperous suburb of Cheetham Hill close to the city centre.

The building opened in 1857.

The exterior was plain but, inside, it was a jaw-dropper, a double cube ballroom 80 feet (24 m) by 40 feet (12 m). This was created by one of the design superstars of the nineteenth century, John Gregory Crace. It had a Louis XV jewel-box interior of gilded curlicues, cornices and cherubs with 20ft mirrors reflecting the light from three stupendous crystal chandeliers.

Getting Crace as interior designer was a coup for the directors of the Assembly Rooms. He had already designed the interior of the Palace of Westminster (Houses of Parliament) with A.W.N. Pugin, elements of the Buckingham Palace interior, the Waterloo Chamber at Windsor Castle and numerous theatres and prominent buildings.

His glittering designs helped make the place immediately popular.

THE ASTONISHING GRANDEUR OF THE INTERIOR

'One of the sweetest events at the Assembly Rooms occurred on 19 January 1870 when 'twenty bachelors of Manchester arranged a fancy-dress ball' for 450 ladies and gentlemen.

The band was Mr. L. Goodwin's and in order that everything might be of the newest and best some of the music had been obtained direct from Vienna and had never been played in England before. Dancing commenced soon after 9.30pm and with the intermission of supper about midnight, was carried on until a late hour yesterday morning.

York Street

After just over a hundred years of entertaining Manchester in splendid style the Assembly Rooms finally failed as the wealthy moved further out of the central areas and deeper into distant suburbs. In 1960 Alderman J. Fitzimons, a former Lord Mayor of the city, bought the buildings but not for music and dancing. He wanted to use them as an extension to his motor tyre business. The crystal chandeliers were a problem though, as Fitzsimons described, they were 'inconvenient' for his type of business.'[13]

Fitzsimons's son said the buildings had to be demolished and had to be turned into a petrol station. There were personal reasons. John Fitzsimons explained how death duties on his father's estate had been crippling and he had to think of the family first. He said: "I hope you don't think we have no feeling in these matters." The Victorian Society called the news 'frightful, the destruction of the building would be a grievous loss to the country'.[14]

ANOTHER OF FITSIMONS' PROPERTIES ADJACENT TO ST. LUKE'S CHURCH

THE PRESTWICH UNION OFFICES

The Prestwich Union Offices were tucked in between the Cheetham Town Hall and the Cheetham Assembly Rooms. They were, in effect, an annexe to the Town Hall. This advert inviting tenders from building companies gives a good description of the intended style of the building:

> *'To Builders and others. The Guardians of the Poor of this Union are prepared to receive TENDERS for the ERECTION of a PUBLIC BUILDING, as Board Room, offices etc.*
>
> *The style will be Italian. The plan shows a central building with two wings, and in the centre of each wing a bay of polished Ashley, carved with ornamental balustrading at the top. The frontage to York-street extends to 43 feet. The cost of the building will be about £1,700.'[15]*

The following year this article appeared in the Manchester Guardian:

> *'PRESTWICH BOARD OF GUARDIANS – Yesterday the members of the board of Guardians for the Prestwich Union met for the first time in their newly-erected offices, York Street, Cheetham Hill Road.*
>
> *The building is situated close by Cheetham Town Hall and has a frontage to York Street of 43 feet. It is in the Italian style and consists of a central building with two wings. On the ground floor are the offices for the clerk to the Board and the other officials as well as a spacious room which is to be used by the Relief Committee.*
>
> *The applicants for relief have provided for them a commodious room, from which, when required to appear before the board, they pass through a small lobby, which commands a full view of the Boardroom, and where, as from a witness box they may communicate with the Guardians.*
>
> *The room in which the general business of the board is to be hereafter enacted is on the upper storey, and extends along the whole front of the building. It is an excellent apartment for the purpose and is comfortably furnished.'[16]*

---

[13] Extract from Manchester Confidential, online news website

[14] Extract from Manchester Confidential's website, by Jonathon Schofield

[15] The Builder 3 August 1861

[16] Manchester Guardian 27 June 1862

York Street

It is interesting to note that, at that time, the use of the terms Cheetham Hill Road and York Street was interchangeable, in fact the building is described as being located at York Street, Cheetham Hill Road.

MANCHESTER UNION WORKHOUSE, NEW BRIDGE STREET

The first Manchester Union Workhouse was built on New Bridge Street in 1792 and opened for 'the reception of the poor' on February 14th 1793:

'A large, spacious, and we may say fairly elegant building. A manufactory of cotton goods is carried out in the house in which the stronger are employed and the children are instructed in the arts of winding, warping and weaving. The average number of paupers of all ages supported by the house is from 350 to 400, whose board costs per head, from three shillings and sixpence to four shillings a week.' [17]

By 1860 the workhouse was home to over 1600 inmates.

In 1855 a new workhouse was erected in Crumpsall to accommodate 1660 inmates. The New Bridge Street building was gradually wound down, although some parts continued to operate until the First World War.

As early as 1875 part of the site was sold to the Lancashire and Yorkshire Railway for an extension to Victoria Station. In 1881 the remaining part of the site was redeveloped with new casual wards, a relief department, female lock (venereal) wards, lying-in wards and lunatic wards.

During the Great War the premises were taken over by the War Office and the buildings were eventually demolished in the 1920s. The land was used as a postal and goods transfer depot. [18]#

---

[17] www.workhouses.org.uk

[18] https://manchesterhistory.net/

York Street

THE FREE LIBRARY AND READING ROOM

The Cheetham Branch Library was opened in 1876, following a competition for suitable designs held in the previous year. This description of the new building comes from the Manchester Guardian:

> *'The library is built of white brick, profusely dressed with white stone, and has a commanding frontage to York Street.*
>
> *Of no particular type of architecture, it comes within the comprehensive title of "classic". The principal features of the front are the arcading of the windows over the entrance, a handsome balustrade which protects the roof and its flanking ornaments of peculiar design.*
>
> *Internally, the library consists of one large room 93 feet long and 59 feet wide and proportionally lofty. The roof is supported by a double row of cast-iron columns, the central portion between the columns being thrown up by a semi-circular principal so as to gain a clerestory.*
>
> *This arrangement, taken with the fact that the three sides of the building which have a street frontage have been pierced with handsome windows, has ensured the thorough lighting of the library.*

> *The book presses have been arranged along the blank wall on the right-hand side from the front doorway. Shelving has been provided for 19,000 volumes and this can be extended at pleasure. A great proportion of the floor space has been arranged for reading purposes.*
>
> *Below the windows along three sides of the room are placed the stands for the newspapers, the central portion being furnished with tables on which will be found the magazines, illustrated papers etc. The total cost is something over £7,000.'*

Modern images show nothing above the balustrade but, whether the additional roof structure, mentioned earlier, ever existed, is not known.[19]

THE NORTHERN HOSPITAL

The history of what eventually became known as The Northern Hospital, has its origins in a small dispensary in the centre of Manchester and ended nearly 150 years later at Alms Hill, Cheetham Hill Road:

> *'The Manchester Northern Hospital was founded in 1856 as the Clinical Hospital and Dispensary for Children, in Stevenson Square. It was the creation of Dr. August Schoepf Merei, a Hungarian in exile, assisted by James Whitehead, a lecturer in obstetrics at the Royal School of Medicine, Manchester and a surgeon at the Lying-in Hospital. Merei was particularly keen to establish a school of research into children's diseases; the focus of the hospital was on research and teaching rather than medical relief.*
>
> *The hospital quickly developed expertise in the growth and development of children. Merei died in 1858, but his work was continued by Whitehead. In 1859, a Ladies Committee was founded. This committee did much work in running the hospital and raising funds, in direct competition with what later became the Royal Manchester Children's Hospital. The early hospital consisted of a dispensary with two beds. More space was needed and, in 1864, land on Park Place, Cheetham Hill Road, was purchased, and a new 25 bed hospital was opened in 1867.*
>
> *Later extensions provided 22 beds for women and 51 cots for children. The hospital was extremely short of funds in the late 1860s, but was helped by the newly founded Hospital Sunday Fund.*

---

[19] See colour picture in the middle section of this book

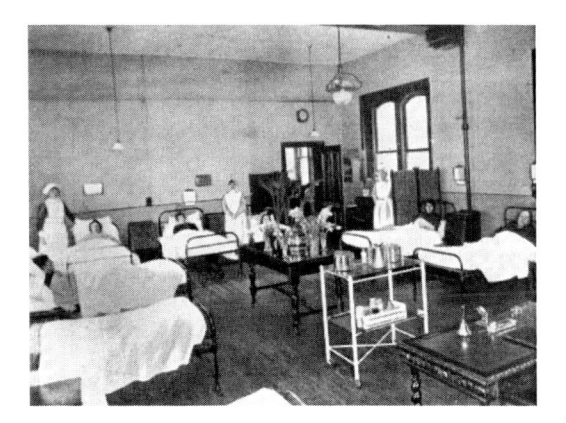

The hospital was originally a children's hospital, but admitted women from an early date. There was a women's department, but it had no in-patients until the 'Whitehead ward' was opened in 1881. In 1882 the name was changed to the Clinical Hospital for Women and Children. The rise in admissions led to the building of a new wing in 1887 and a large extension in 1892 gave the hospital a frontage on Cheetham Hill Road. The first woman surgeon was appointed in 1900.

The name of the hospital was changed again in 1902, to the Manchester Northern Hospital for Women and Children. Despite extensions and the building of a new operating theatre in 1909, there was a growing realisation that the hospital building was out of date.

A decision was made in the 1920s to build a new hospital on Alms Hill, where a site had been given by Sir Edward Holt. However, due to a lack of finance, the hospital did not open until 1934. With the advent of the NHS in 1948, Manchester Northern Hospital became part of North Manchester Group. The hospital became a general hospital, admitting male patients. Most of the children's beds were transferred leaving only 11 children's beds. The hospital closed in 1994.'

CHEETHAM BATHS AND PUBLIC HALL

Cheetham baths were built in 1892 and remained in use for over 80 years until they were replaced by the new facilities at the Abraham Moss Leisure Centre on Crescent Road in 1973.[20]

---

[20] It is worth noting that by 2010 the new facilities were to be replaced, having survived for only half as long as the older baths

York Street

The baths were at the lower end of the building and the Public hall at the higher end. The first-class pool could be covered with a wooden floor and used as a gymnasium during the winter months.

There was an impressive tower which housed a public clock. There were twenty slipper baths and a residence for the baths' superintendent above the ticket office.

The two photographs below reveal a curious structure attached to the baths.

In the second photograph, there is a massive structure attached to the side of the clocktower, even obscuring the face of the clock on that side. This appears to be a set of very tall chimneys, supported by metal ties. It is just possible to make out a set of shorter chimneys in the same position in the older photo. It had been planned for the boilers to be in the centre, between the baths and the hall, so the reason for these chimneys is uncertain. Possibly the plans were changed and the boilers were placed at the end instead. There may have been a problem with the smoke dispersal because of the proximity of the tower. Whatever the reason, the chimneys were certainly not there by the time the building was demolished.

RYECROFT HOUSE

Ryecroft House stood in extensive grounds on the corner of Seymour Road. This extract from the Manchester Evening News from around 1995 tells of the death of its most famous resident:

> 'More than a 100 years ago townsfolk were saddened at the news of the sudden death of Edmund Salis Schwabe while on holiday in Canada.
>
> Flags were hoisted at half-mast at the Rhodes Works, Middleton Liberal and Conservative Clubs, Rhodes New Bleach Works (Messrs. O. Ashworth & Co.), Rhodes bowling green and the cricket ground.

York Street

Their mood changed to disbelief when the full details were later published in this newspaper. Salis Schwabe the senior partner of the extensive Rhodes Works which employed more than 1,000 workers, lived at Rycroft House. Eighteen months prior to his untimely death he suffered an attack of gout and depression, a condition that would result in his demise.

Mr. Schwabe, a well-known and respected employer by the workforce for his ability to supervise the day-to-day affairs of the factory, he was frequently seen with his two brothers, constantly on hand to enlarge the business making it a success. To lift his spirits, he decided on taking in a world tour. Visiting India, China and Japan in the company of a companion and a medical advisor.

Salis, aged 50, a widower for 20 years, was on the homeward journey staying at the Windsor Hotel, Montreal. Early in the morning of 4 August 1891 a gentleman occupying the adjoining apartment heard the sound of a single gunshot. On entering Mr. Schwabe's room he found him in a state of unconsciousness with a bullet wound to his head.

Despite immediate medical treatment he expired soon afterwards, he left a daughter to mourn his loss. At the inquest the jury returned a verdict of suicide while in a temporary state of insanity.

Edmund Salis Schwabe will be remembered for his generosity; Little Heaton School, the now demolished reading room and library are testimonies.

A quiet and unassuming man he was keen to promote education, he gave a generous subscription towards establishing a library at Owen's College, Manchester.'

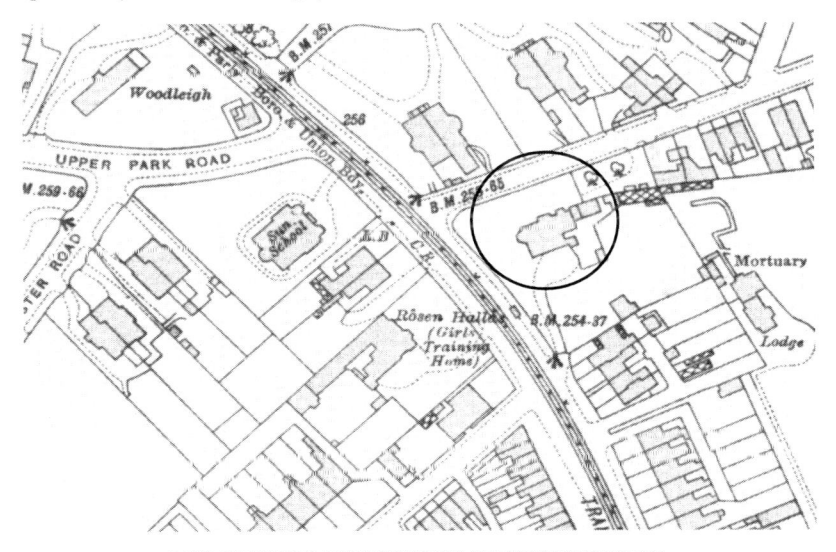

MAP SHOWING THE LOCATION OF RYECROFT HOUSE

STOCKS HOUSE AND FARM

Stocks, or Stocks House as it was called in different periods of its history, stood opposite the end of Dirty Lane, now Elizabeth Street. Before the length of Cheetham Hill Road extending from New Bridge Street to Stocks was made the road to Cheetham Hill from the town was along Long Millgate, over Scotland Bridge and up Red Bank. (then by North Street to Dirty Lane).

As to the origins of the name 'Stocks' or the extent of the estate connected with the house little is known. In Green's Plan of Manchester and Salford, published in 1794, Stocks is depicted as being a short distance past 'Mile House,'[21] The estate appears to have extended about 130 yards east of the high road, and to have been about the same length from north to south.

---

[21] Later, The Mile House public house

York Street

The outbuildings were numerous and the grounds were laid out in an ornamental manner with gardens, shrubberies, ponds and walks. One lake was serpentine in shape and about a hundred yards long, and appears to have been connected with the ornamental waters in Strangeways Park. In the centre of the plan of the Stocks estate is the name of J. Rydings, Esq the surrounding fields being marked as the Earl of Derby's.

At the time referred to (1794) Stocks was a fine, roomy mansion, one portion of which was three storeys high and another two storeys. It stood some little distance from the road, and just past it were the stables with the turret, which last named still survive, although devoted to a very different purpose from that for which they were intended.'[22]

For over two hundred years members of the Rydings family lived at Stocks, first in an earlier house and later in the grand mansion, which was built around 1750. There are entries in the Collegiate church registers from 1573 to 1806.

The map here, dating from around 1857, shows that the grounds were, at that time, still both extensive and elaborate, with the serpentine lake clearly visible.

Around 1830 - 40 Mr. Gilbert Winter was the resident there. He may have been the owner or he may still have been leasing the property from the Earl of Derby, as the Rydings family had done.

Gilbert Winter was a very successful wine merchant and a Boroughreeve of the town.

He was a director of the Liverpool and Manchester Railway and the first meetings of the directors were held at his offices in St. Anne's Street. The two Stephensons, father and son, were often seen there.

We have already heard that at the time when Mr. Gilbert Winter was the owner, Stocks House was frequented by many rich and famous visitors and that on one occasion Charles Dickens was introduced to two local worthies, the Grant Brothers, whom he immortalized as the Cheeryble Brothers in his novel Nicholas Nickleby.

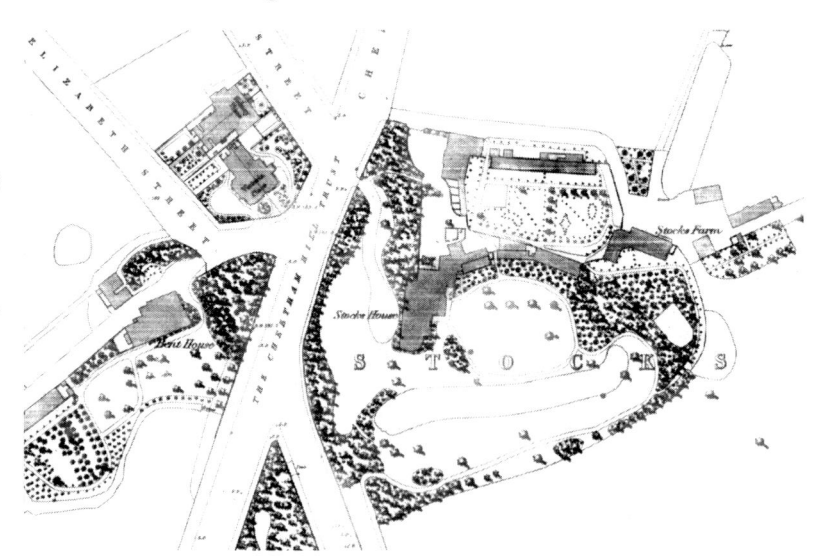

Prior to that time the house was the property of John Ridings, a merchant and manufacturer. The last owner of Stocks House was James Crossley[23] and, after his death it lay abandoned for a few years before being demolished.

Stocks farm survived for almost another 100 years. In the 1920s it was the premises of a building company, Messrs. H. Green and Son, who were the primary contractors for the building of St. Matthew's Sunday School on Delaunays Road, Crumpsall in 1922.[24]

---

[22] Manchester Streets and Manchester Men, T. Swindells

[23] See page 21

[24] See the image in the colour section in the centre of this book

York Street

FERNACRE AND ALMS HILL

The entire area to the North of Cheetham Hill Road from Smedley Lane to where is now Greenhill Road was occupied by just three large mansions. The smallest of these was Fernacre which stood on a triangular plot of land between Alms Hill and the main road:

> 'In the middle years of the nineteenth century in Fernacre House lived one of the proprietors of Harrop, Taylor and Pearson, a large silk mill. At that time, Newton Heath was a centre of silk weaving and this company's mill was the largest of several in the town, employing over 3,000 operatives.'[25]

Alms Hill had various uses during its time. When St Luke's Church was built it was the home of the Rector. Later it became a girls' school and had a farm attached. It was also used for a time by the First Manchester Rifles for drill practice on Wednesday evenings.

At the side of number 48 Manswood Drive the remains of a boundary wall can be seen. This was the eastern edge of the Rectory property. Before the surrounding houses were built the rectory would have had a commanding view over the area and the notion of the HILL of Alms Hill would have been much clearer.

The estate to the west, where the house itself stood, has the imaginatively named Abbotsfield Court, although there is no evidence of any such clerical connection.

TEMPLE SQUARE

The square was built as a result of The Addison Act, designed to address the issue of sub-standard housing. At the onset of the First World War, it became a cause of concern to the government that many of the men who were called up to join the army, and who came from areas of sub-standard housing, were unfit to serve. After the war those returning from the front had expectations that they would be looked after by the government.

The expression 'Homes Fit for Heroes' was coined by a newspaper headline writer to convey, in a short, easily-digested sentence, the content of a speech which the Prime minister, David Loyd George had made.

Across the country, affordable housing, making the best of limited resources and man power, were designed and built, with many of them surviving to this day.

They all had inside bathrooms, at least two bedrooms and, in some cases, a pantry.

One such group of houses was built on spare land, adjacent to The Temple, further perpetuating the name in Temple Square. On the front of Cheetham Hill Road a block of tenement flats was also built at around the same time.

The author's Grandparents were among the first to move into Temple Square on its completion. They lived at number 9, an upstairs flat. This had internal stairs leading from what was classed as the front door, facing into the square, and an outside staircase, leading to an outside toilet and small balcony at the back, facing Queens Road.

The entire square was renovated in the 1980s including all the houses and flats being re-roofed. A large stone monument was placed in the centre of the square with a plaque, explaining how it came to be built.[26]

---

[25] Broughton and Cheetham Hill in Regency and Victorian Times, Monty Dobkin

[26] See picture in colour section in the centre of this book

York Street

QUEENS ROAD TRAM AND BUS DEPOT - Boyle Street

'In June, 1899, the "Cars, Sheds and Staff Sub-Committee" of the Manchester Corporation Tramways Committee was looking for a site for one of the largest electric tramcar sheds in the country, as part of the Corporation plans to take over and electrify the existing horse-tram network of the Manchester Carriage & Tramway Company.

The site was purchased from Lord Derby, and in June 1900 the Chairman of the Tramways Committee, Councillor Daniel Boyle, after whom Boyle Street is named, laid the foundation stone.

The tram shed cost £90,000, and was built to house 252 tramcars. Although it was officially opened at the start of the City's first electric tramcar service on 6th June, 1901, new trams had been stored in the unfinished building, and some were damaged in a fire in April of that year.

Tramcars entered the building through four entrances off Boyle Street, and one at the corner of Queens Road, which has since been bricked up.

In the late 1920s, express bus services to supplement the tramcars were introduced. These express buses served Norden and Gatley, and Altrincham and Hyde, via the City Centre, running in addition to the tramcars and charging higher fares. A motorbus garage was erected in 1926-28, at a cost of £17,332-8-6 to house these vehicles.

This building now forms the Upper Hall of the Transport Museum, and traces of the original vehicle inspection pits can be seen in the floor.

By the mid-1930s, the motorbus fleet was expanding rapidly, and the electric tramcar was out of favour with the City's Transport Committee. An increasing proportion of the tram shed was used for garaging motor buses until the last tramcar left in 1938.

In 1934-35, a bus washing and fueling bay was erected between the bus garage and the tram shed, and the area was roofed over at a cost of £7,218-16-6.

Ambitious road schemes planned during the 1960s envisaged both Queens Road and Cheetham Hill Road being rebuilt as multi-lane dual carriageways, with a large intersection at their junction. Fortunately for the appearance of the district, many of these plans did not come into being and the modern houses on Queens Road and the older ones on Cheetham Hill Road underwent a programme of refurbishment once the blight of the road plans was lifted.' [27]

---

[27] Extracts from the website of the Manchester Transport Museum

York Street

JOSEPH HOLT'S BREWERY, DERBY STREET

This timeline is comprised of a few extracts from the History of Joseph Holt's Brewery as described on their own website

> '1849 Brewing starts. After moving into small house in central Manchester, Joseph starts his brewing career at a premises in Oak Street, in the Northern Quarter.
>
> 1855 Ducie Bridge Brewery. In the first major expansion, the Holt's take over Ducie Bridge Brewery on York Street, now Cheetham Hill Rd, brewing ales and porters.
>
> 1860 Derby Brewery move. Joseph Holt takes out a 999-year lease on a piece of land where he begins work on the brewery from which the company still operates today.[28]
>
> 1861 First pub acquired. After just supplying beer to local pubs, the brewery acquires the Wellington Hotel in Eccles - the first pub under Joseph Holt.
>
> 1908-1909 Edward Holt twice elected Lord Mayor in successive years
>
> 1914 Manchester & District Radium Institute. Alongside leading scientists, Edward establishes the new Radium Institute. This was later amalgamated with Christie's Hospital
>
> 1955 Woodthorpe Hotel opens. The home of the Holts since 1884, the Woodthorpe opens its doors as a hotel.
>
> 1960 King William IV in Salford closes but the bar survives and finds itself in the Rover's Return.'

The brewery has continued to thrive and is now a well-recognised brand both in Manchester and further afield.

---

[28] See picture in colour section in the centre of this book

CHAPTER V – SMEDLEY, THE FORGOTTEN SUBURB

There is a point, around where the tollgate at Alms Hill Road once stood, where Cheetham Hill Road veers westward, leaving the edge of the Irk Valley, and heading off towards Bury and beyond.

Perhaps the wealthy property owners wanted to keep in touch with the open aspect towards the distant Pennine hills and so they began a new spur of development along what is now Smedley Lane, at right angles to Cheetham Hill Road.

I include this area because of the importance of the residents who lived there and its close proximity to the main road.

Despite the many important people who lived here in former times, Smedley seems to have slipped through a crack and have been forgotten sometime in the past. Its near neighbours, Crumpsall, Cheetham, Collyhurst, Harpurhey and Blackley are all familiar names to most residents of Manchester, but you don't hear anyone say 'I come from Smedley' or 'I live in Smedley' It truly seems to be The Forgotten Suburb of North Manchester.

It may come as no surprise, therefore, to read this definition of the place name;

> English (mainly Nottinghamshire): apparently a habitational name from *a lost or unidentified place,* perhaps so called from Old English smeðe 'smooth' + leah 'wood', 'clearing'

Maybe it was always destined to be forgotten?

There are hints, of course to remind the passer-by of its existence; Smedley Lane, Smedley Road, the playing fields and the pub are well enough known, but the area itself is harder to pin down.

What is more interesting, however, is the fact that this small, insignificant corner of the great City of Manchester was home to many of the greatest figures in our history; writers and adventurers, clerics and bankers, benefactors and malefactors lived, often side by side, in close proximity to each other.

And before them all, did the tramp of marching feet echo in its valley as Roman Legionaries passed through on their way north to Ribchester?

Turning the corner from Cheetham Hill Road, the first, and at one time the most imposing, building to be encountered on Smedley Lane is St. Luke's Church;

If you were to go back to this earlier time, when there were open fields as far as Prestwich and the railway had only just sliced its path through the side of the Irk valley, you would find Smedley in bold letters on the map, in larger, more impressive letters than its near neighbour Harpurhey.

Many of the houses along Smedley Lane were built by the merchants whose wealth was created by the development of Manchester as the world's first Industrial City.

They chose 'the countryside' far enough from the pollution of the industry they'd created, but close enough to be able to visit their manufactories on a regular basis and keep a close eye on things. Others were the homes of bankers and men of the cloth, among whom were magistrates and other 'elders' of the city authorities.

Let us look, then, at some of the houses and their occupants. T. Swindells, writing in 1908 gives us this description of Smedley Lane:

> *'Although Smedley Lane retains a certain amount of semi-rural appearance, things were very different there when St. Luke's Church was built (1839). Behind the church, standing in the middle of fields was Smedley Cottage, and a little distance beyond on the same side was Beech Hill. Between the grounds of Beech Hill and Smedley Hill was a farmer's road leading to the fields.'*

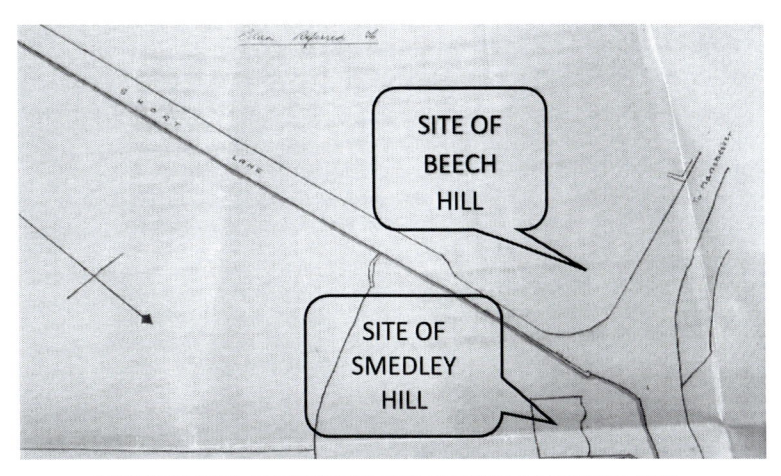

SHOWING THE FARMER'S TRACK IDENTIFIED AS 'SHORT LANE'

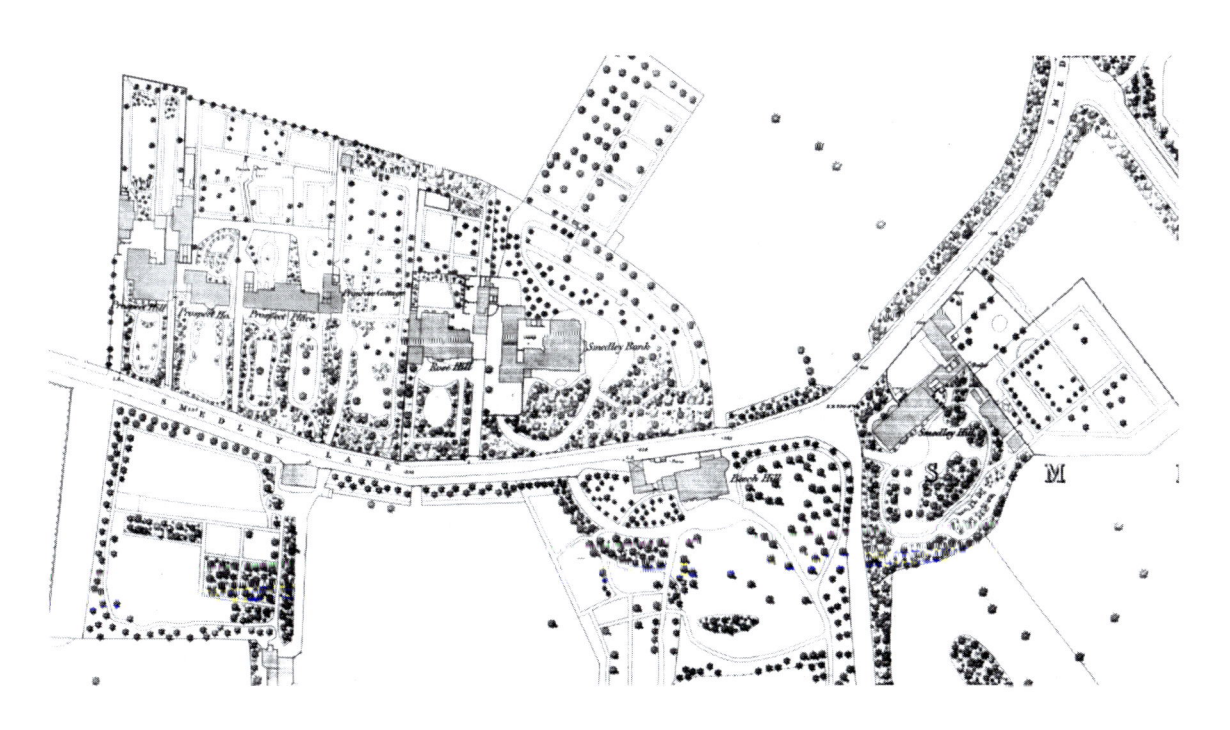

DETAIL MAP SHOWING THE LARGE HOUSES ON SMEDLEY LANE

BEECH HILL

John Chippindall – calico printer and father of the first Rector of St. Luke's Church – lived at Beech Hill.[29]

His son, the Rector, was also called John but he had a brother, Edward, with a very interesting story. The following extracts are from the records of Archives+ at Manchester Central Library[30]

---

[29] See, also, William Harrison Ainsworth

[30] https://manchesterarchiveplus.wordpress.com/tag/edward-cockayne-chippindall

York Street

'Edward Cockayne Chippindall was born in 1853 in a small village in Staffordshire. His grandfather, described his occupation as 'Esquire'.

Edward went to sea and by the time of the 1871 census, aged 17, while his family were in Cheetham Hill, he was a midshipman aboard the Eclipse in the Royal Navy but by the end of the year he had been promoted to a Sub Lieutenant.

He was awarded a Certificate of Competency as a Master of the Merchant Navy for him in 1873, from

From 1873 he became involved with a captain Thomas Haynes, whose occupation, as stated on his daughter's wedding certificate, was 'Explorer'.

A report in the Lancaster Gazette dated 4th September 1880, says that Edward was now in Fiji, where he was tried for the manslaughter of a 'native.

His father wrote a heartfelt plea on his behalf, saying that the charges had been made up by the Governor of Fiji, Sir Arthur Gordon (Later of Khartoum). Edward had somehow become entangled in a dispute of some kind with him.

After a long and drawn-out sequence of events the Magistrates in Fiji threw the case out.

In 1881 he was involved in a shipwreck of the ship ZARA, once owned by Captain Haynes.

Although Edward managed to save the crew, the ship was beached but then broke up.'

The book 'Pearls and Pearling Life' by Edwin Streeter (a jeweller of Bond Street, London) dated 1886 tells us that Edward and the Captain are shown to be heavily involved in the pearl fishing industry in Australia and the islands. Streeter funded their exploration in far off islands and colonies. He said that the pair faced many perils, including a mutiny.

Their ship, the Sree Pas Sair, was once described as a 'charnel house' and on one occasion, on venturing to land on a small island, they were surrounded by 'hundreds of canoes with armed savages in them'. There is no explanation as to how they managed to escape from this somewhat dangerous encounter.

And so, we finally arrive at Broome Bay.

Edward and the Captain continued to explore and expand the industry - one report states that they owned 2 schooners and 11 luggers.

However, tragedy struck Edward whilst he was on board the schooner *Telephone.* He died of 'brain fever' on 22nd May 1886 while at sea and he was brought back to Broome Bay and interred in the aptly named Pioneer Cemetery.

Back home in Smedley Lane a fine memorial to him was erected at St. Luke's Church.

York Street

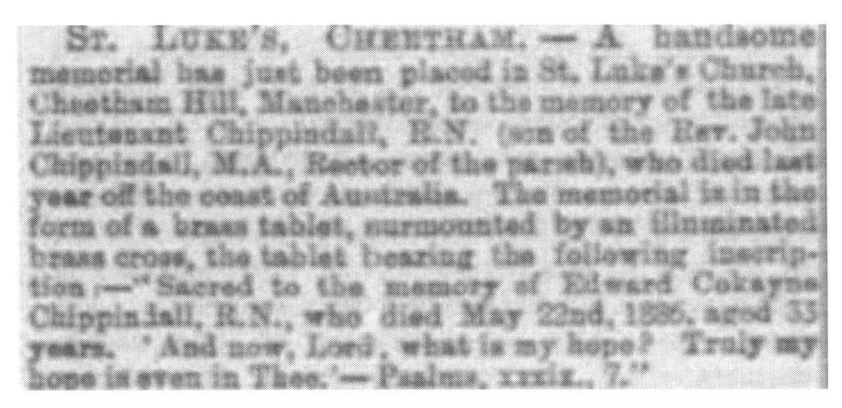

> ST. LUKE'S, CHEETHAM. — A handsome memorial has just been placed in St. Luke's Church, Cheetham Hill, Manchester, to the memory of the late Lieutenant Chippindall, R.N. (son of the Rev. John Chippindall, M.A., Rector of the parish), who died last year off the coast of Australia. The memorial is in the form of a brass tablet, surmounted by an illuminated brass cross, the tablet bearing the following inscription :— "Sacred to the memory of Edward Cokayne Chippindall, R.N., who died May 22nd, 1886, aged 33 years. 'And now, Lord, what is my hope? Truly my hope is even in Thee.'— Psalms, xxxix., 7."

Incidentally, the intrepid explorer, Captain Haynes, continued to work in Australia for many years, but obviously returned to England from time to time as he fathered 7 children! He died in 1929 in England, aged 76 leaving a large amount of money (£16,600)

But the story has one final, intriguing twist

When he died, even though his wife and seven children were still alive, his cremated remains were shipped to that isolated pioneers' cemetery, where he was laid to rest beside his friend and partner Edward, Cockayne Chippindall – together once more.

Haynes' great grand-daughter provides some further information about the Pearl Fishing venture:

> 'In Roebuck Bay he organized the clearing of a passage through the mangrove swamps and built the first rough jetty. This site was later chosen for the first township of Broome, although in 1888 it was nothing more than a village, some pearling luggers, several shanties and some local Aborigines.
>
> Streeter set up a store trading in pearls and mother of pearl shell and built the famous Roebuck Hotel. The store and the hotel are still standing. In 1911 a disastrous cyclone destroyed everything and he was forced to return home. Thomas spent many years around north Western Australia and left instructions that his ashes should be returned to Broome. His eldest daughter recalled that the ashes had to have their own cabin on the voyage and that the cost was £50'.

STOWELL MANOR[31]

The first house after Cardinal Street (formerly Church Street) on the north side of Smedley Lane was once the home of Reverend Hugh Stowell, a flamboyant figure who preached at St. Luke's Church and Christ's Church, Salford and who soon developed a reputation as a 'vigorous and inspiring preacher'.

He was not a stranger to controversy and often came up against the Roman Catholic congregation in Manchester.

---

[31] This house was originally called Prospect Hill and formed a trio of grand villas along with Prospect House and Prospect Place. Since it had been the home of Hugh Stowell and, when it was renovated, in recent years, the developer gave it the name in recognition of its historical connections

> *'Hugh Stowell (3 December 1799 – 8 October 1865) was a Church of England clergyman. He graduated at Oxford in 1822, and took holy orders the following year.*
>
> *He held various offices in his Church; became rector at Salford in 1831; was appointed honorary Canon of Chester Cathedral in 1845, and later Rural Dean of Eccles.*
>
> *He published several volumes. He also edited a book of hymns: A Selection of Psalms and Hymns Suited to the Services of the Church of England, 1831.*
>
> *He was an implacable opponent of Catholic emancipation whose supporters built Christ Church in Salford, Lancashire, for him, where he remained from its consecration in 1831 until his death.*
>
> *Stowell gained 'national notoriety' as a consequence of the Hearne v Stowell libel case brought against him in 1840 by Daniel Hearne, a Catholic priest.*

This account is from 'The Story of the Old Faith in Manchester':[32]

> *'Father Hearne was a very active missioner, and won the affections of his large Irish congregation by incessant labours for both their temporal and spiritual welfare. He had, however, had one bitter antagonist in the Rev. Hugh Stowell.*
>
> *At a meeting that was held in Manchester in 1840 to petition Parliament against making any further grants to the Catholic Seminary, Maynooth College, Dublin, Mr. Stowell made a gross attack on Catholicity, and singled out Father Hearne.*
>
> *He quoted a case of one of Father Hearne's penitents, John O'Hara, being seen crawling about in Smedley Lane on his hands and knees, performing the penance imposed on him by his Confessor. The poor penitent was afterwards proved to be out of his mind – a harmless maniac, ignorant of what he was doing.*
>
> *Father Hearne sued Mr. Stowell for libel.*
>
> *A vast amount of interest was taken in the trial which resulted in a unanimous verdict being returned by the jury in favour of Father Hearne.'*

O'Hara was known to be insane and was not called as a witness, Stowell's defence claiming that whatever a clergyman said in the performance of his duties was not libelous so long as the clergyman believed it to be true. Stowell was found guilty and ordered to pay damages of 40 shillings, a decision that was reversed on appeal.

SMEDLEY BANK (BANK VIEW)

This was the residence of the Rev. Canon Cecil Daniel Wray, who died there in 1866. He wrote 'Early Recollections of The Collegiate Church':[33]

> *'When I first came to Manchester in 1809, the Sunday Morning Lecture always commenced in the nave at six o'clock. The bells tolled at five and at half past five and then at six Mr Brookes or myself were always at the reading desk ready to begin the litany. The attendance at these early morning services ranged from 200 to 300 persons.'*

---

[32] By John O'Dea 1910

[33] This is Manchester Cathedral

York Street

In 1847 when he preached the anniversary sermon in Chethams Hospital, he was approached by George Pilkington who remarked that there was no statue of Humphrey Chetham and offered £200 'or as much as would be necessary' to provide one. The result was the statue we can see now.

Canon Wray took a prominent part in promoting the Ten Hours Bill and was often seen in company with the Earl of Shaftesbury,[34] Lord John Manners and other leaders of the movement.

> *'Canon Wray was a popular if somewhat eccentric priest who served the Collegiate Church for 56 years. He was a contemporary of Joshua Brookes[35] and a rival to the claim of being the most prolific baptiser and 'marrier' in English history.*
>
> *Records show that he presided over 33,211 christenings, 13,196 marriages and 9,996 funerals as a result of the massive growth in population during the Industrial Revolution.*
>
> *Canon Raines describes how Wray would turn up at the cathedral in a carriage and four, with liveried footmen; he would bow to the Dean, shake his fellow Canons by the hand and then proceed to shake the hands of the Minor Canons with two fingers, and to curate he would present a single finger.*
>
> *On the occasion of his 88th birthday he set up a fund for the provision of socks for the poor on his birthday each year.'[36]*

He is buried in the Cathedral churchyard, and his Sock Appeal continues on his birthday each January.

On an early map the name is given as Smedley Bank. However, the gate posts are engraved Bank View. It is uncertain when and why this change occurred, but at the time it was built it would certainly have commanded the best view of all the houses on the north of Smedley Lane, as the ground dropped steeply beyond it down to the Irk valley below.

SMEDLEY HILL

The Rev. Charles Wickstead Ethelston lived here. See the section about St. Mark's Church in the following chapter.

WILLIAM HARRISON AINSWORTH.

Ainsworth was born on 4 February 1805 in the family house at 21 King Street, Manchester, to Thomas Ainsworth, a prominent Manchester lawyer, and Ann (Harrison) Ainsworth, the daughter of the Rev. **Ralph Harrison**, the Unitarian minister at Manchester Cross Street Chapel.

Ainsworth read romantic works as a child and enjoyed stories dealing with either adventure or supernatural themes. Of these, Dick Turpin was a favourite of Ainsworth.

During his childhood, Ainsworth began to write prolifically.

The Ainsworth family moved to Smedley Lane[37] during 1811. They kept the old residence in addition to the new, but resided in the new home most of the time.

---

[34] Shaftesbury Road runs at right angles to Cardinal Street and parallel to Smedley Lane

[35] Joshua Brookes was immortalised in 'The Manchester Man' by Mrs G. Linnaeus Banks

[36] Taken from the website – 'Canon Wray's Sock Appeal'

[37] Beech Hill, also, later, the home of the Chippindall family, already mentioned

The surrounding hilly country was covered in woods, which allowed Ainsworth and his brother to act out various stories.

His writing, however was not universally admired. Edgar Allan Poe described the style of writing as 'turgid pretension'.

GUY FAWKES: Ainsworth relied heavily on historical documents describing the trial and execution of the conspirators, of whom Fawkes was one, but he also embellished the known facts.

He invented the character of Viviana Radcliffe, daughter of the prominent Radcliffe family of Ordsall Hall – who becomes Fawkes's wife – and introduced supernatural elements into the story, such as the ability of the alchemist, John Dee, to raise the spirits of the dead.

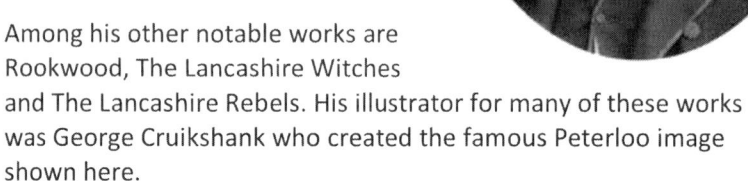

Among his other notable works are Rookwood, The Lancashire Witches and The Lancashire Rebels. His illustrator for many of these works was George Cruikshank who created the famous Peterloo image shown here.

GEORGE CONDY, HENRY CONDY AND CONDY'S FLUID

George Condy, originally from London, lived at Smedley Lane.[38] He was a barrister who became editor and joint proprietor of the Manchester and Salford Advertiser, and a commissioner in bankruptcy. He had few equals as a critic of music, painting and drama.

His son, Henry, took after his mother and developed a keen interest in chemistry.

---

[38] Address unknown

York Street

'In 1659 a German chemist, J. R. Glauber was the first person to produce potassium permanganate. Just over 200 years later Henry Bollman Condy was developing an interest in disinfectants, and had marketed several products including ionised water. He had pursued a different path of research to Glauber and he produced a compound which he called Condy's Crystals or Condy's Powder. Since his compound was so similar to potassium permanganate, he spent considerable time and money in litigation to prevent his competitors imitation his crystals

Tender Feet, hot feet, tired feet, instantly relieved by bathing in "CONDY'S FLUID." Cheap, safe. Directions with bottle. Sold everywhere. Refuse imitations.
Use "Condy's Fluid."

In 1857 Condy patented 'Condy's Fluid' which had the advantage that it could be used both externally and internally. It was produced in the family factory in Battersea, London.' [39]

Advertisements that appeared in the Kingston newspaper **The Gleaner** during the 1860s and 1870s claimed that Condy's fluid was used in many ways, as follows;

- To prevent the communication of Infectious Diseases
- To purify Sick Rooms and the Wards of Hospitals and Crowded Places
- To disinfect water
- To purify Stagnant Water
- To purify cattle and dog yards and where offensive matter lies about
- To ensure Purity of Water employed for drinking - which frequently contains much organic matter
- To purify fever wards or - in cases of death from a contagious disease - to prevent offensive effluvia arising from a dead body
- To deprive Night-chairs[40] of offensive odour
- To purify the atmosphere of Rooms in which there are Dead for the Visits of Undertakers and Jurymen
- To purify Bilge Water in a Ship's Well To parity with the Interior or Hold of a Ship
- To extirpate from Fowl-Houses and to preserve the health of Fowl
- To disinfect the soil while emptying Cess-pits

Such a product must have been indispensible in its day. However, far from being a 'secret solution' it appears that it was simply a common household disinfectant consisting essentially of a solution of potassium.

TROOPS WALKING THROUGH CONDY'S FLUID BATHS

---

[39] Extracts from Wikipedia

[40] Presumably commodes

York Street

JOHN RYLANDS - entrepreneur and philanthropist

(7 February 1801 – 11 December 1888). He was the owner of the largest textile manufacturing concern in the United Kingdom, and Manchester's first multi-millionaire.

In 1825 John Rylands married Dinah, the only daughter of W. Raby, of Ardwick Green and although retaining lodgings in Manchester, he fixed his home in Gidlow Lane, Wigan.

As increasing business required him altogether in Manchester, he removed in 1834 to a house in Smedley Lane, whither his wife and children accompanied him. A few years afterwards he took a town house in Newton Street, but he still kept his country house at Smedley.'[41]

In connection with his residence at Smedley he would humorously tell a characteristic little incident:

> *'He had to walk home through a low district, and once having had a pocket-handkerchief taken out of his pocket, he devised a plan by which to catch the thief.*
>
> *Tying a piece of string to one corner of the handkerchief, and passing the string through his sleeve, he held it in his hand while sauntering through the locality where he was sure the article had been stolen before.*
>
> *As soon as the rogues were at their old game he, feeling the pull at the string, turned round, immensely to the surprise of the thief!*
>
> *The plan was answered, for he never lost a handkerchief again.'*

EUSTRATIO RALLI – merchant

There were five Ralli brothers: Zannis (a.k.a. John) Augustus, Pandia (a.k.a. Zeus) Toumazis and Eustratio.[42] Between them they founded Ralli Brothers, perhaps the most successful expatriate Greek merchant business of the Victorian era.

Born to a wealthy merchant family of the island of Chios, their father Stephenos Ralli (1755–1827) had settled in Marseille, but recognized that the nexus of trading had changed in the aftermath of the Napoleonic wars, and sent his eldest son John to London to explore business opportunities.

Later, the brothers expanded their business empire with a move to Manchester.

> *'They were quick to seize new opportunities created by wars, political events, and the opening of new markets, such as corn, cotton, silk, opium and fruit, rapidly establishing major trading operations across the Mediterranean, Russia, reaching out as far as St. Petersburg, Taganrog, Tabriz, Alexandria, Smyrna, and Syria.*
>
> *Although they employed more than 40,000 people at one time, control rested in the hands of the extended family.*
>
> *From 1851 Ralli Brothers started operations in India with offices in Calcutta and Bombay that specialized in jute, shellac, teelseed, turmeric, ginger, rice, saltpetre, and borax, with 4,000 clerks and 15,000 warehousemen and dockers.*

---

[41] Extract from Wikipedia

[42] He also lived at Beech Hill, Smedley Lane

They made fortunes by building on the Indian and American businesses, astutely shipping cotton and textiles after the American Civil War and, from 1882, dealing in opium. From new offices in Pondicherry and Madras they dealt in 'Khandesh' groundnuts. When World War I started, Rallis held the exclusive contract with the British War Department for jute sandbags.'[43]

The imposing Ralli Building, boasting seven floors stood for many years on the banks of the Irwell, on the Salford side, and was only demolished in the 1980s.

NATHAN LASKI - SMEDLEY HOUSE

'Nathan Laski was born in 1863. He joined a cotton exporting company at a young age, frequently visiting India as part of his duties, and went on to develop it considerably. Although the son of an immigrant, he was keen to distance himself from immigrant culture. Involving himself in communal affairs from his twenties, Laski was the president of the Great Synagogue in 1896, and went on to become president of the Jewish Board of Guardians. He was also the first provincial Jew to serve as an officer on the national Board of Deputies of British Jews, and in 1906 he was made a Justice of the Peace.

As the "uncrowned king" of the Jewish community, Laski held court at Smedley House, Smedley Lane. People queued for his help and advice, and it has been estimated that he saw over 70,000 such visitors during his lifetime. He was an imposing and intimidating figure, a stubborn man who was used to getting his own way.

He initially opposed the building of the Manchester Victoria Jewish Hospital as something that would prevent immigrant Jews integrating into British society. Later, however, he accepted the position of chairman of the Jewish Hospital and remained there for 20 years until he was struck by a car on Cheetham Hill Road in 1941.

Ironically, he died a day later at the same Jewish Hospital. Another example was his antagonistic attitude towards political Zionism, which softened considerably after the Balfour Declaration (1917).

Politically, Laski was President of the North-West Manchester Liberal Association and in 1904 he pledged his support for Winston Churchill's bid to become MP. Churchill had made a show of opposing the Aliens' Act, which had limited immigration into Britain at a time of Russian and East European persecutions, and which was passed by Balfour's Tory government in 1905. As a result, Churchill won the election, and Laski became a lifelong friend.

It was at one of Laski's dinners that, despite his dislike of Dr Chaim Weizmann, Churchill and Weizmann first met.

Laski's two sons were Judge Neville Laski, KC, and the economist Professor Harold Laski of the LSE and a Chairman of the Labour Party NEC. After WW2 Neville donated Smedley House to become the first Manchester Jewish Home for the Mentally Handicapped, now at Brookvale in Simister Village.'

---

[43] Extract from Wikipedia

York Street

A Humorous postcard from Cheetham Hill

Horse trough at the Half Way House Junction

St. Luke's Church

Early advertising for the Penny Bazaar

York Street

The Manchester Jewish Museum with its proposed extension

The Manchester Ice Palace, Derby Street

Picture postcard with views of Cheetham Hill Road

York Street

Joseph Holt's Brewery, Derby Street

What remains of the Cheetham Boundary marker on the side of the Derby Brewery Arms

York Street

View along Cheetham Hill Road towards St. Luke's Church with Brideoak Street to the right.

Architect's plan for the free library showing the roof detail above the balustrade.

CHAPTER VI - PLACES OF WORSHIP AND EDUCATION

ST. MARK'S CHURCH

Prior to 1794, the next parish after the Collegiate Church in Manchester, had been that of St. Mary's in Prestwich. The gradual development of Cheetham as a township in its own right meant that there was a need for a new 'chapel of ease' to be established.

T. Swindells tells us:

> *'This chapel, was built amongst the cotton merchants' houses which formed that desirable hamlet.'*

Despite its relative importance - at the time of its construction it was regarded as the third most prominent church in the parish of Manchester architecturally it was considered insignificant:

> *'St. Mark's is about the most unpretentiously ugly building in the United Kingdom, a horrid brick structure, which would be complimented by being called a barn, and which was built in the heathen period of the Church of England, when the chief gods worshipped in the island were ugliness, cheapness, cockfighting, bull-baiting, brandied wines and the devil in various other shapes.'*[44]

The Rev. Charles Wickstead Ethelston became the first minister at the church of St. Mark's Cheetham which was built largely at the expense of his father Rev. E. Ethelston.

T. Swindells tells us:

> *'This chapel, was built amongst the cotton merchants' houses which formed that desirable hamlet.'*

He took up his position at St. Mark's at the age of 27, remaining until his death on September 14th 1830 aged 63. He was a man of letters and wrote a volume of verse. When, in the early years of the nineteenth century, the Manchester and Salford Corps of Volunteers was formed (in response to the threat from France) he was appointed their Chaplain and consecrated their colours in the Collegiate church.

Ethelston is perhaps better known, however, for his role in The Peterloo Massacre than for his work as a minister at St. Mark's.

There is a great deal of confusion about the reading of The Riot Act at Peterloo. Some say it was read by Parson Hey, of Rochdale, others state that no-one read it at all.

However, this article (source unknown) seems to definitively place the responsibility firmly on the shoulders of Ethelston and one other magistrate:

> *'As the reading of The Riot Act has been by many disputed, it may not be amiss to state (although the Magistrates do not see it forming any necessary feature in the case) that the Proclamation was read twice before the apprehension of (Henry) Hunt, by the Rev. C. W. Ethelston from the upstairs window of Mr. Buxton's house, and by Mr. Sylvester from the ground.'*

Suffice it to say, Ethelston's presence is undisputed, and there is strong evidence to suggest that it was he who read the fateful words.

Whether or not anyone in the vast crowd was aware of the reading is a discussion which will continue, perhaps, for another 200 years.

---

[44] From an article printed in The Sphinx about 1870

ST. MARK'S SUNDAY SCHOOL

Close to the church, on St. Mark's Lane, a Sunday School was built, opening in 1815. This was demolished sometime in the nineteen eighties, but the builders of the property which replaced it had the presence of mind to preserve the foundation stone and incorporate it in the new exterior wall.

The church's 225th anniversary was marked by a small ceremony when flowers were laid at the church by the current incumbent Rev. Sarah Hartley, representatives of the City Council and the group Friends of St. Mark's[45] who are working to renovate the churchyard and make it a community asset.

ST. MARK'S PRIMARY SCHOOL

There being no available land closer to the church, St. Mark's Primary School was built a little distance away, on Heath Street.

In keeping with the plain construction of the church, the school was an unprepossessing building of stock brick with a small, walled playground. Built in 1902 it lasted almost one hundred years before being replaced by a new school on Halliwell Lane in 1990. This change may have coincided with the demise of the Church and its local parish, as it was amalgamated with Trinity Church.

ST. LUKE'S CHURCH

St. Luke's, an Anglican Parish Church, was begun in 1836 and completed in 1839. It is constructed of ashlar in the Perpendicular Gothic style, designed by T. W. Atkinson. There is some confusion as to how the church was paid for. One source describes it as a commissioners' church,[46] whilst in several other places, as below, we are told that the money was raised by local subscription:

> 'The foundation stone was laid Wednesday June 29th 1836 and the church was consecrated on Sunday 6th October 1839.
>
> The cost of £23,000 to build the church was raised locally and it was built on land given by the Earl of Derby. It was regarded as one of the finest examples of church architecture in Manchester.
>
> It had 1,250 seats, 500 of which were free from pew rents.
>
> The organ was consecrated by the fingers of Felix Mendelssohn, who played it in 1847, the year of his death when he visited Manchester to give a performance of his 'Elijah'. It is also believed that Charles Dickens attended the consecration ceremony.
>
> St. Luke's attracted a fashionable congregation, but towards the end of the 19th century its decline commenced as people moved further from the city centre.'[47]

---

[45] Visit Facebook page 'Friends of St. Mark's Cheetham' for further information about this group

[46] A Commissioners' church, also known as a Waterloo church or Million Act church, is an Anglican church in the United Kingdom built with money voted by Parliament as a result of the Church Building Acts of 1818 and 1824

[47] Extract from Wikipedia

York Street

The following article gives a little more detail about the construction:

> *'St. Luke's Church in Cheetham Hill, Manchester – now, sadly, mostly demolished – has always been regarded as one of Thomas Atkinson's best church designs.*
>
> *Like so many of Atkinson's other ecclesiastical buildings, it was what is referred to as a Commissioner's Church, completed in 1839 with money received from the French as reparations for the Napoleonic Wars and designed to accommodate the growing number of worshippers to be found in the rapidly expanding industrial towns of the north.*
>
> *It was built of ashlar (finely worked masonry) in the Gothic Perpendicular style that Atkinson helped to popularise and originally it could accommodate a congregation of more than 1500.*
>
> *Bellhouse, who is known to have designed parts of the Manchester New Workhouse and who was a member of The Ecclesiological Society, is fulsome in his praise of Atkinson's building. "I consider the design and execution of the edifice alluded to be of such high excellence, that it is only doing a bare act of justice to the architect to whose genius we are indebted for this beautiful work of art, and to the admirers of modern ecclesiastical architecture, to give a greater publicity to it than it has yet received.*
>
> *I am happy in being able to state that the finishing and painting of this beautiful church was entrusted to the care of Mr. Atkinson. The whole of the walls are tinted of a warm stone colour, the mouldings left white, and the most prominent members of them gilt, which gives it a most rich and mellow appearance. The ceiling over the nave is divided by the roof principal. The pews are painted to imitate grained oak, and lined with crimson moreen.'*

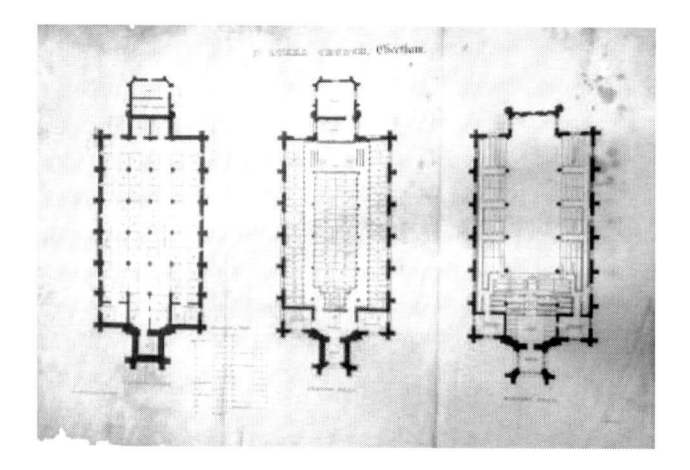

It was said that the railings around the church and its grounds were amongst the finest in the land. Sadly, these are now in a poor state of repair and, in some areas, they are missing entirely.

ST. LUKE'S SCHOOL

There was a small school attached to St. Luke's. This was one of the first Board Schools[48] and, in time, became a school with a high reputation, verging on the status of a Grammar School.

Little is known of the history of the establishment, other than to say it was held in high regard and the teaching staff expected its pupils to achieve high standards.

---

[48] William Forster's Elementary Education Act 1870 required partially state-funded board schools to be set up to provide elementary (primary, in modern parlance) education in areas where existing provision was inadequate. Board schools were managed by elected school boards

York Street

It is described in this picture as a 'Higher Grade' board school which meant that it had pupils up to the age of thirteen, and not, as is usual today, just to eleven.

ON THIS MAP ST. LUKE'S SOUTH OF THE CHURCH AND TEMPLE SCHOOL IS THE ONE TO THE EAST.

THIS WAS A TEMPORARY STRUCTURE AND WAS REPLACED WITH A NEW SCHOOL TO THE SOUTH OF THE PICTURE HOUSE

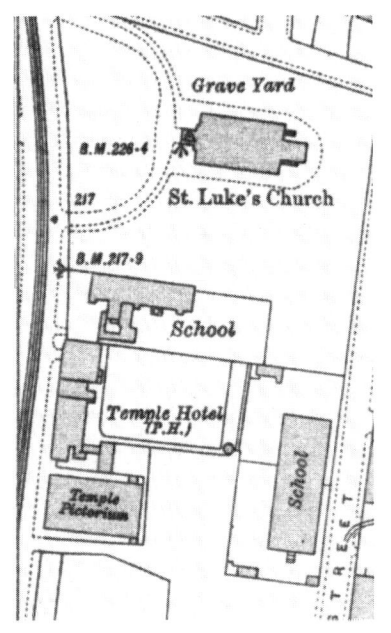

St. Luke's Higher Grade Board School, Cheetham Hill, Manchester. 1883—1894.

TEMPLE SCHOOL.

From the map above the first Temple School can be seen as a small block lying along Boyle Street. This was a temporary structure which was replaced a short time later with a bigger school which lay at right angles to it and, at the same time, Smedley Street was created.

By 1922 the school had a long frontage facing south. This was a two-storey building with both Infant and junior departments. On the ground floor there were verandas with large doors which could be opened to allow fresh air into the classrooms.

Due to its proximity to the predominantly Jewish area of Cheetham Hill, many of the pupils were Jewish and the school catered well for them and allowed the children to celebrate the Jewish holidays in addition to the Christian holidays which would normally be observed.

In 1972, the author completed a Teaching Practice at the school. At that time, the headmaster was a Mr. Hayton. In his office there hung a photograph dated from the late 1950s showing a row of fifty-six children, ranged in size from tallest to shortest and beneath each child was inscribed their nationality. Fifty-Six different nationalities in one school, such was the cosmopolitan flavour of Cheetham Hill Road.

The 1920s building was replaced with a new school, The Temple Academy building on Smedley Lane in 1999. The site of the old school has been largely built on, with a small area retained as a playing field for the school.

York Street

SMEDLEY BANK SPECIAL SCHOOL

On the opposite side of Smedley Street, or the corner of Cheetham Hill Road stood Smedley Bank Special School which appeared, at least, to have been built at the same time and in the same style as Temple School. This was a smaller school created at a time when education philosophy believed that children with special needs should be extracted from schools and taught in a separate environment.

When this policy changed, and 'inclusion' became the watchword, almost all Special Schools were closed and reintegrated into the education system for other purposes. Smedley School became an annexe of Temple School, allowing it to expand, and accept a greater number of pupils.

ST. CHAD'S CHURCH

In 1847 St. Chad's church was built close to Manchester to serve the expanding Roman Catholic population. The first St. Chad's had been started in a small room overlooking the River Irwell near Parsonage Gardens and then moved to premises on Rook Street[49] near Mosley Street.

A detailed history of the church can be found in the book 'St. Chad's – Parish and People' written by the author and published in 2006. An edited and revised edition was published in 2019 with the title 'St. Chad's Cheetham – Mother Parish of Manchester'.[50] This omits a large section containing extracts from the Parish Log Book. The following information is taken from that book.

Mgr. Philip Hughes, a Catholic historian describes the development of the parish:

> *'For nearly fifty years this first St. Chad's endured. Then, since it threatened to fall down from disrepair, for a time, it ceased to be used except for Sunday Mass.*
>
> *Marriages were still celebrated there, but baptisms were administered at St. Augustine's until, in 1828, with the appointment of Rev. Thomas Maddocks as head priest, the chapel in Rook Street returned to the fullness of its old life.*
>
> *With the appointment as head priest in 1835 of the Rev. William Turner, the chapel became once more the centre of Catholic life in Manchester.*
>
> *But the inconvenience of its poor accommodation and the heavy expenses its tumbledown condition continually entailed, led the clergy to think first of re-building, and then of rebuilding on a new site.*
>
> *A purchaser was found for the old site and, after several failures, the present site was at last secured in 1845.'*

---

[49] There are descriptions of a rookery in trees in a garden on nearby Spring Gardens which may be the origin of the name Rook Street

[50] Available from www.all-things-considered.org

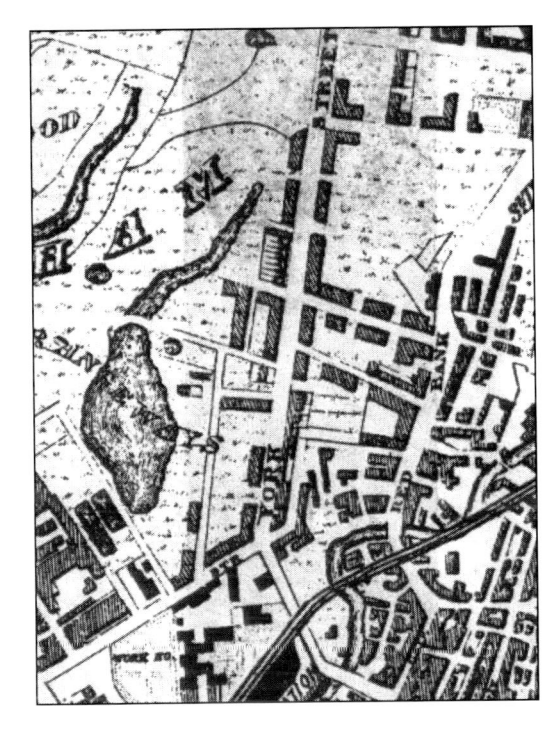

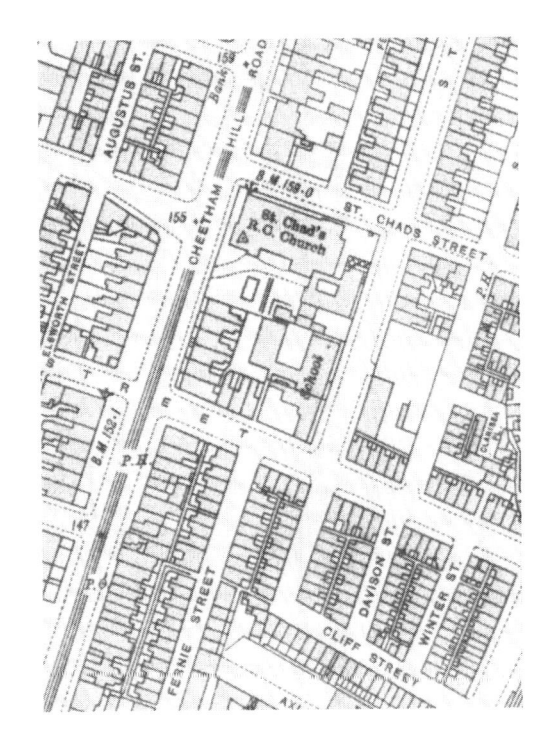

THESE TWO MAPS SHOW THE STARK CONTRAST BETWEEN 1847, WHEN ST. CHAD'S WAS BEING BUILT

AND 75 YEARS LATER WHEN THE WHOLE AREA HAD UNDERGONE MASSIVE DEVELOPMENT

ST. CHAD'S SCHOOL

The first school at St. Chad's occupied the remainder of the plot of land between the presbytery and Lord Street on one side and from Stocks Street at the back to Cheetham Hill Road at the front. Built of the same stone as the church it was itself a fine edifice.

In the 1960s, slum clearance removed the vast majority of the housing in the immediate vicinity of the church, replacing it with wholesale and manufacturing premises.

As the housing disappeared it also became necessary to consider the provision of schooling at St. Chad's. The old building which had served the parish so well for 125 years was falling into disrepair and, since the population of the parish was now centred a mile or more up Cheetham Hill Road, beyond Elizabeth Street, it became apparent that a new school was needed.

THE SCHOOL WAS THE BUILDING TO THE LEFT OF THE WHITE LINE, THIS PHOTOGRAPH WAS TAKEN IN 1966

THE DEMOLITION OF THE OLD SCHOOL

York Street

NOTRE DAME CONVENT, BIGNOR STREET

The Sisters of Notre Dame originally founded their convent in Stocks Street, close to St. Chad's church, and had close ties to that parish throughout the period of their existence in Cheetham Hill.

The order had been founded in France in 1804 as a teaching order and in 1845 the congregation made their first excursion into England, setting up a school in Penryn.

In April 1851 Fr. M. Sheehan, from St. Chad's approached the sisters to establish a school in Manchester:

> *'Application having been made by the Rev. M. Sheehan from St. Chad's, Manchester, in order to obtain Sisters of Notre Dame for his mission, Sister Marie Alphonse de Ligouri and myself were desired by our Reverend Mother to go to Manchester to see the house destined for our sisters and make all necessary arrangements... The house was still occupied... but we went to see the church and also the buildings raised for the schools, both for boys and girls. The former if a fine Gothic edifice.'*[51]

The sisters remained in Stocks Street until 1893 when an opportunity arose to buy the former Cheetham Reform Club on Bignor Street. It was decided to buy the property, for £1,250 – the headmistress's salary at that time being 18 shillings and sixpence per week.

Pupils of the school will have been aware of the history of the building as the doors to the chapel bore the monogram of the Reform Club 'CRC'

THE CONVENT AND SCHOOL VIEWED FROM THE GROUNDS

VICTORIA WESLEYAN METHODIST CHURCH

'The first of a series of services in connection with the opening of the new Victoria Chapel (Wesleyan), at the corner of Queen's Road and Cheetham Hill Road, was conducted in the chapel, yesterday afternoon, by the Rev. Luke Wiseman, President of the Wesleyan Methodist Conference.

The new chapel is one of the most important erected by the Wesleyans in the North of England. Messrs. Clegg and Knowles, of Manchester, are the architects, under whose direction the works already executed have been carried out. The chapel only is built at present, but the committee confidently hope that in a short time funds will be forthcoming to enable them to complete their scheme.

The entire design comprises a chapel, lecture room, three classrooms, and a chapel-keeper's house. The chapel is roofed over in one span, without intermediate pillars. Dormer windows have been placed on each side of the roof, and afford ample light and enhance the architectural effect. Equal attention has also been given to the acoustic properties of the building, the form of roof, being the one best adapted to ensure certain success in that respect.

---

[51] From the website of the Society of Notre Dame

York Street

The three doorways at the west end open to a spacious vestibule, divided from the chapel by a handsome glazed screen, and communicating only with the tower and north staircase. A space for the organ and choir is placed in a separate recessed gallery, behind the pulpit, divided from the chapel by a lofty arch with granite shafts and moulded stone corbels. A gallery also extends along each side and one end of the chapel. 490 sittings are provided on the ground floor, and 340 in the galleries. Pitch pine, carefully selected and well varnished, has been used for all the fittings. The east and west windows are filled with stained glass.

The general contract has been carried out by Mr. Mark Foggett. The chapel is warmed by a hot-air apparatus. The cost of the chapel and all its fittings is estimated at £5,500, of which about £3,200 has been promised or received in the shape of voluntary contributions, and £1,840 has been obtained by a bazaar and various other means. The new chapel will be used by the congregation formerly worshipping in Ebenezer Chapel, Red Bank, which is to be used in future as mission chapel for working men'[52]

The chapel closed in 1950. It was eventually demolished and a group of maisonettes was built on the site.

The location of the Ebenezer Chapel is uncertain, but it is likely to have been the building shown here as a synagogue, and the hall behind, which may have been a Sunday School. Adjacent is Ebenezer Place.

The Public House marked is The Queen's Arms, Honey Street.

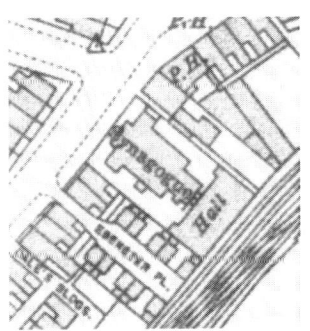

DUCIE WESLEYAN CHAPEL

It was founded in 1840 but only lasted 50 years as a chapel, closing in 1892. It was then taken over by the Jewish community who opened it as the Central Synagogue in 1894.

In later years it became the premises of Laidlaw and Thompson, a well-known Manchester ironmongery firm and, in most recent times, it has had various incarnations as a furniture store, a bed warehouse and an immigration centre and solicitors' offices.

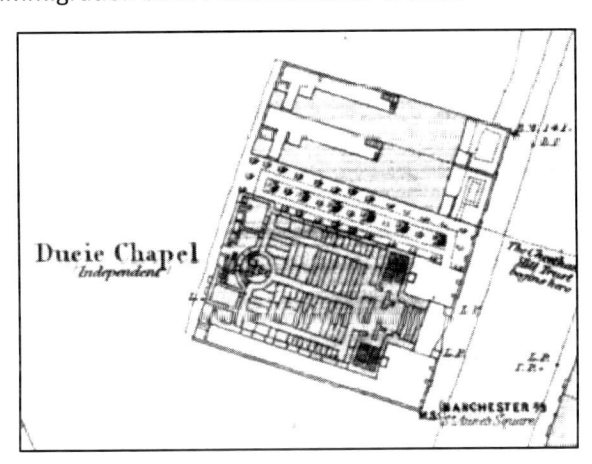

---

[52] The Manchester Times – Saturday 07 December 1872

York Street

ST. MARY'S UKRAINIAN CATHOLIC CHURCH

Situated on Cheetham Hill Road, close to its junction with Middleton Road and Leicester Road.

It is under the jurisdiction of the Apostolic Exarchate for Ukrainians in Great Britain of the Ukrainian Greek Catholic Church.

Originally the church was the Sunday School building for The Parish Church of St. John the Evangelist, Broughton, until it was bought by the Ukrainian community. Prior to that they had held services at St. Chad's Roman Catholic Church.

CHEETHAM HILL WESLEYAN METHODIST CHURCH

Adjacent to the Half Way House, on Cheetham Hill Road, stood Cheetham Hill Wesleyan Methodist Church a large edifice built of red sandstone[53] and with an impressive spire:

> 'A commanding site at The Polygon was secured containing over 9,000 square yards. The foundation stones were laid in 1894 and in April 1896 the new church was opened. In addition to the main body of the church there was a lecture hall, ladies' parlour and commodious vestries.'[54]

The site of the church is now occupied by Anchor Court, sheltered accommodation, although the impressive boundary wall has been retained.

TRINITY UNITED CHURCH

The church, generally known as Trinity Church, is listed on the diocesan register as Cheetham United Church. In addition, it now forms part of a group with St. Thomas's, Lower Crumpsall, and the former St. Mark's Cheetham under the supervision of one minister.

This extract, written for the centenary of the present building, has been provided by the current incumbent, Rev. Sarah Fletcher:

---

[53] It is possible this came from the sandstone quarry in Collyhurst

[54] Extract from 'Cheetham Hill Circuit Jubilee 1863 – 1913'

York Street

'Trinity Church has had a varied life. The congregation was originated by the Presbytery of Belfast in 1843. Rev. John Dickson was ordained as its first minister and served from 1843 to 1845, when the Belfast Presbytery transferred the congregation to the Lancashire Presbytery of the Presbyterian Church of England.

The congregation had obtained a site on New Bridge Street in Manchester, and a Church and schoolroom were being built. Rev. William McCaw was ordained and inducted as Minister of the Church on December 1st 1846 and served for nearly forty years. Together with Mr. J. Armstrong, Mr. Thomas C. Morton and Mr. William Ferran, who were elected by the congregation as Elders they formed the first session of Trinity Presbyterian Church.

Towards the end of the 1800s a great many of the members were moving out to other districts and the area was becoming more industrialised. It was felt that the site of the church needed to be moved. Steps were taken for the Church and the site to be sold and this was finalised in May 1898.

Temporary premises for worship were arranged in the Conservative club on Cheetham Hill Road. This stood on the corner of New Elizabeth Street which is now lost beneath the Manchester Fort retail park.

A new site was bought, the site of the present building, about one and a half miles from New Bridge Street

The Church and schoolrooms were opened for worship on Sunday October 14th 1900 by Rev. George Hanson D.D. of Marylebone, London

CONSERVATIVE CLUB ON THE CORNER OF NEW ELIZABETH STREET

The Church endured a period of uncertainty when there was no incumbent Minister but, when Rev. F. Coop was appointed, he brought new life to the congregation, especially in the early part of the Great War. After the ministry of Rev. P. M. Paton ended in 1948 the Church was served by a succession of interim Moderators. In the late 1950s alterations were made to the building, making a smaller area for worship and creating a hall for badminton and other social uses.

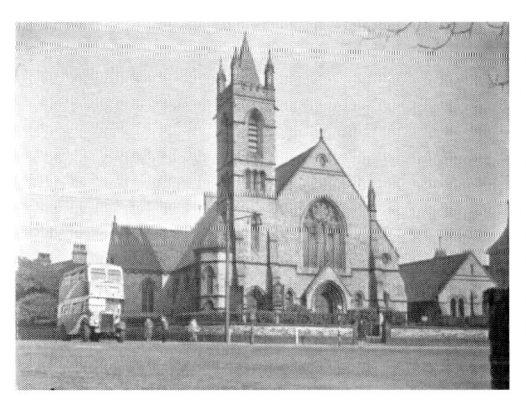

In 1972 the Presbyterian and Congregational Churches came together to form the United Reformed Church. Trinity became one of the member churches of the North East District of the North West Province.

In 1978 Rev. Fred. Thomson, who was Minister at Alkrington United reformed Church, became Minister at Trinity and a joint Pastorate was set up with Alkrington, which has proved very helpful, and a good fellowship between the two Churches has developed.

St. Luke's, whose Church was at the corner of Smedley Lane, had to be vacated. The members of that Church started worshipping at trinity in 1977 and, gradually, the two congregations united and started working together to become a Local Ecumenical Partnership in 1981. An Ecumenical group – The Jesus People, also joined in at this time, although this group has now moved away.

Other groups have used the building for worship – this being Trinity's contribution to making the building available for all in the community.

One hundred years of worship, witness and service which we now celebrate have continued from this building. Who knows what sort of varied life will occur in the future? Let us hope that Trinity will rise to the occasion.'

York Street

CHEETHAM CONGREGATIONAL CHURCH

This small church was situated between Cheetham Hill Road and Brideoak Street, with the entrance to the Sunday School being on the latter.

In 1972, it combined with the Presbyterian Church at Greenhill Road to form the Trinity United reformed Church.

HEATH STREET SCHOOL

The school on Heath Street went through many different incarnations over its lifetime.

It was erected in 1894 with the name Cheetham Higher Grade School (teaching pupils up to the age of 13). It was later known as Cheetham Central School – a secondary school taking pupils from the surrounding primary schools, such as Temple, St. Mark's and Crumpsall Lane.

In its final incarnation as a school, it was known as Heath Street Secondary Modern School and was finally replaced when the Abraham Moss High School was built

For some time in the late 1960s and early 1970s it was also the home of evening classes for adults.

THE KHIZRA MASJID

This mosque is part of UKIM – The United Kingdom Islamic Mission. The UKIM is one of the oldest nation-wide Islamic organisations in the U.K. It was founded in October 1962 on the initiative of a small group of Muslims who used to meet at the East London Mosque in a study circle. They discussed the need of forming an organization in Britain to convey the message of Islam in the West.

Today, from this small beginning, the UKIM has expanded to about forty-five branches and circles in the UK and around thirty mosques and Madaris. The activities, which the UKIM is involved in, are diverse, from building new mosques, relief work, to Dawah on the Internet and youth work.

Attached to the UKIM complex is the Educe Academy which offers courses in a variety of subjects, such as TESOL and Child Care, with online courses and access to the Open University. They also offer translation and interpretation services.

York Street

THE NORTH MANCHESTER JAMIA MOSQUE

*'The establishment of the mosque commenced in 1975 by **Qamaruzzaman Azmi**, an Islamic thinker, orator, and writer. Azmi began giving Dars-e-Quran at Shah Jalal Mosque (1A Eileen Grove, Rusholme) near Wilmslow Road, Manchester by travelling from Bradford every week.*

At that time, there were few Sunni Mosques in Manchester. Within a short period of time, the Victoria Park Mosque appointed a Sunni Imam.

In 1979, the North Manchester Jamia Mosque started off under the leadership of Azmi at 25 Bellott Street, Cheetham Hill, Manchester which was a house converted into a mosque. As the facilities at this building were very limited and the growing population of Muslims needed facilities for Islamic activities on a larger scale, a plot of land was purchased in 1982 and the first phase of the mosque, consisting of the main prayer hall providing prayer facilities for 1,200 men and women, was completed in 1984. The second phase consisting of a College of Islamic Studies and additional prayer facilities for 1,200 people was built in the 1990s.

The current third phase of the project is a major complex that will allow the mosque to hold prayer facilities for up to 10,000 people, a community hall, Imams' residence, a mortuary, office, library, and guest rooms. Since its establishment, it remains the primary Muslim organisation in the north of Manchester and a focal point for the Manchester Muslim community.'[55]

ARCHITECT'S IMAGE OF THE FINISHED COMPLEX

JEWISH SCHOOLS

'The Manchester Hebrew Association had founded religion classes by 1838. In 1842 they established a school in Halliwell Street but moved to larger premises on Cheetham Hill Road in 1851. Once again, in 1869, the school moved to larger premises, this time in Derby Street and became known as the Manchester Jews' School.

Cheetwood School opened in 1889 and, by 1907, 80% of the pupils attending were Jewish.

Heath Street School also catered for the Jewish population and Hebrew was taught from 1915.'[56]

---

[55] www.manchestermasjid

[56] From the Manchester City Council website

York Street

The building with the square tower on the top in this photograph is where the Jewish School was established in 1851. It stood a few doors away from The Pleasant Inn, in the area now occupied by The Green Quarter:

THE SCHOOL ON DERBY STREET WITH ITS UNUSUAL ROOFTOP PLAYGROUND

CHEETHAM HILL ROAD SCHOOL

THE TALMUD TORAH SCHOOL

'The Talmud Torah School was a school for the teaching of elementary education in Hebrew, the Scriptures and the Talmud and in the principles of the Jewish faith and practice.

Talmud Torah schools were traditionally for boys only. Girls were admitted in modern times. The School was founded in 1880 and established in purpose-built premises at No. 11 Bent Street, Cheetham, Manchester. In 1958 the Bent Street school was sold'.

The street to the side of the building was named Torah Street. On the corner of this street was a textile company. The employees there would, cruelly, wave rashers of bacon out of the window at the boys coming and going to the school.[57]

KING DAVID SCHOOL

The large complex which exists today began as a small Primary School building in the late 1950s.

This stood on Seymour Road and occupied the site of one of the large houses which stood in Wilton Polygon. At the time the school was built, there were still several of the old houses still standing.

Over the ensuing decades the school gradually expanded, first with the building of a secondary school between the Primary school and Eaton Road and then, by further expansion onto the rest of The Polygon, until it occupied the whole site from Grey Street to Polygon Road.

The school is consistently rated amongst the highest-achieving schools in the country.

The circular drive which led to the front doors of the mansions is still visible today, as a walkway between the school buildings.

---

[57] As related by Bill Williams on his guided tours of the Jewish Quarter

York Street

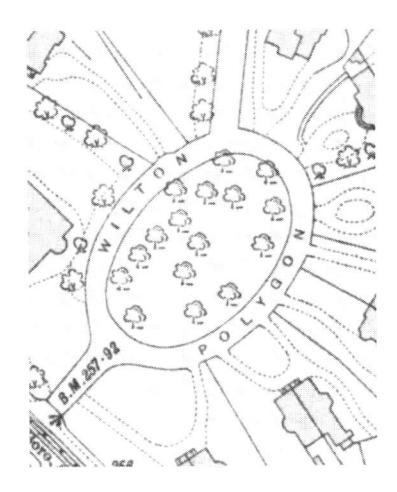

ROSEN HALLAS - The Manchester and Salford Boys' and Girls' Refuge and Home

To the west of Cheetham Hill Road, and just north of George street stood the Rosen Hallas Home:

> 'This organisation was founded in 1870 by Leonard Kilbee Shaw and Richard Bramwell Taylor. At first it concentrated on destitute boys, offering them a bed for the night and a meal.
>
> In time it branched out into a fully campaigning organisation bringing neglectful and abusive parents to court and running holiday homes as well as seeking to provide work and training for young people and emigrating some of them to Canada.
>
> In 1878 it opened the first girls' home at number 12 George Street and then added number 2 – 10 along the same row. A little later it added the Rosen Hallas Home which was an impressive building, standing in its own gardens and having a small hospital in the grounds.
>
> Here they looked after 30 – 40 older girls who "came voluntarily, stayed willingly and were free to leave after due notice".
>
> There were many success stories and many of the girls "have responded to the influence brought upon them while at Rosen Hallas Home.

Some were difficult cases, often owing to their misfortunes rather than to their fault because of their earlier associations, and their difficulties have been a challenge to the love and patience of those weaving good character from the raw material of neglected childhood". [58]

SYNAGOGUES

To describe in any detail the various diverse groups within the Jewish community would take up too much room in this volume. However, Bill Williams does the job admirably in his book 'Jewish Manchester, an Illustrated History'. Chapter 5 describes how small, discrete groups first created small 'Chevroth', often in the back yard of their lodging houses, where a small group would gather for religious observances.

---

[58] Adapted from the 'Forever Trust' website

York Street

In time Jews of similar persuasions from these individual Chevroth gathered their resources and created larger Chevroth and, eventually, the first synagogues. I would heartily recommend this book to anyone wishing to study this aspect in greater depth.[59]

For anyone wishing to identify the location of a particular building there is an excellent website to help.[60]

BILL WILLIAMS 1932 - 2018

SOME OF THE SYNAGOGUES OF CHEETHAM HILL ROAD

THE GREAT SYNAGOGUE

THE NEW SYNAGOGUE

THE UNITED REFORM SYNAGOGUE

---

[59] Jewish Manchester, an Illustrated History – Bill Williams 2008. ISBN 978-1-85983-615-6

[60] www.jewishgen.org/jcr-uk/Community/man_addresses.htm

York Street

THE SPANISH AND PORTUGESE SYNAGOGUE – Now the Manchester Jewish Museum

'On 4 February 1872, Manchester's growing Sephardi (Jewish people from Spain and Portugal) community met to discuss building the first Sephardi Synagogue in the city. Two years later our synagogue opened – on 6 May 1874. The Sephardi community thrived and by 1904 a second Sephardi synagogue was built in south Manchester.

Over the years our synagogue has changed to reflect the needs of the congregation. In 1919 a plot of land was purchased at the rear of the synagogue to create a new succah (temporary hut constructed for use during the Jewish festival of Sukkot). Complete with a sliding roof, this 'succah building' became permanent and was used as a Congregational Hall. It is now our learning studio and kitchen.

In 1913 former Synagogue President, Ezra Altaras, passed away. His family paid for a large memorial window to commemorate him. This memorial window now sits proudly over the Synagogue's Ark. Following this, other families paid for similar memorial windows on the ground floor. We now have over 40 magnificent stained-glass windows, many of which depict biblical scenes.

By the 1970s the congregation was moving out to the suburbs and the synagogue membership was starting to wane. The last wedding took place between Jeremy Colman and Deborah Hodari on 25th September 1977.

During this time a Jewish heritage committee was formed and local historian, Bill Williams, appointed to write The Publication of the History of Manchester Jewry. *The idea of converting our synagogue into a museum was first broached by Werner Mayer, it's then President in 1976.*

The Jewish Heritage Committee, which later became the museum's first board of trustees, was formed and launched a public appeal to raise funds to convert the synagogue into a museum. In 1982 the synagogue's congregation moved to a new building on Moor Lane, Salford and building work began on the new museum.

After two years of conservation work our museum opened on Sunday 25 March 1984 with a temporary exhibition The Making of Manchester Jewish Museum. *A new permanent exhibition opened a year later.'*[61]

Such is the success of the museum that after 35 years it is to undergo a major transformation.

It will be doubled in size and the exhibition space will allow a much fuller display of the museum's collection and scope for visiting exhibits throughout the year.

There will be catering facilities and meeting and gathering spaces in a purpose built extension to the west of the original synagogue, which itself will undergo a major renovation and refurbishment, with further conservation work to its original features.

---

[61] www.manchesterjewishmuseum.com/collections/synagogue-story/

CHAPTER VII – ENTERTAINMENT AND LEISURE

THE GRIFFIN HOTEL – Public House[62]

The Griffin, along with the adjacent public hall, formed the entertatinment hub for this part of Cheetham Hill, whilst the Cheetham Assembly Rooms and Cheetham Town Hall served the same function closer to the town centre.

The present building replaced an earlier one of the same name and on the same site. In 1820 a charity ball was held to raise funds for St. Mark's Day and Sunday School and almost 300 people attended. Wheeler's Manchester Chronicle gave a vivid description of the event:

> 'Present at the event were the rank and fashion of that genteel neighbourhood, of several adjacent towns and of Manchester and Salford.
>
> As the whole scheme of the undertakling was founded on charity and, consequently, in economy, the Stewards and the Committee felt that they owed much of their success to the exertions of their amiable partners. The supper, the wines and the dessert were to be gratuities, and thirty families of the vicinity supplied all these in the most abundant quantities.
>
> The sum of one hundred guineas has been obtained, and has resulted in the liquidation of a debt contracted in building the school.
>
> Six rooms of the large inn were used for dancing, cards, promenading, refreshments and supper. On the following day the rooms were opened for the gratification of the working classes of Cheetham Hill and the neighbourhood, to whom the surplus provisions of the preceding night were liberally distributed. On Sunday, each child educated in the school was complimented with a bun – thus, in the end, the rich and poor were combined in one common feeling of satisfaction on the occasion.'

The school rooms had been completed in 1815 and, when the premises were finally demolished in the mid-1980s the foundation stone was rescued and incorporated into the side of the new warehouse, built in its place, on St. Mark's Lane.

In 1836 The Ladies of the Parish were busy again and held a fundraising bazaar in the schoolrooms.

The list of patronesses gives a clear insight into the families of wealth who were living in the area at that time.

John Chippendall was a calico printer, whilst his son, also John, was Rector of St. Luke's for nearly 40 years. C. W. Ethelston, a magistrate, had been a prominent figure at Peterloo in 1819. Mr. Halliwell had built properties and developed the lane which came to bear his name, whilst the Winters, of Stocks House, were well-known not just locally but also further afield. Gilbert Winter was a wine merchant, a boroughreeve of Manchester and a close friend of the Stephensons, the railway pioneers.

Whilst the men were busy establishing their fortunes the womenfolk occupied their time raising money for good causes in the community.

---

[62] Now Bhatti Fabrics

York Street

The Griffin was one of several pubs along Cheetham Hill Road which had a bowling green attached. In addition, it also boasted a quoiting ground (seen here on a map from 1851).

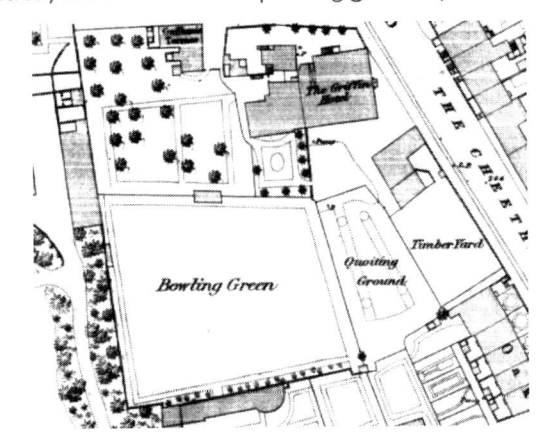

A TYPICAL QUOITING TEAM OF THE PERIOD

The game was most popular in northern parts of Yorkshire and Northumberland and the rules were not standardised until 1881. Players toss rings at a stake, called the hob. A ring that encircles the hob scores two points for the thrower; a ring closer to the hob than an opponent's scores one. The rings are usually made of iron and weigh about three pounds, but rope or rubber rings are also used.

Why there should have been a quoiting ground in Cheetham Hill, as early as the 1850s, is something of a mystery.

THE TEMPLE – Public House[63]

The Temple has strong historic connections with the Peterloo Massacre:

> 'On the Cheetham Hill Road there was formerly an old hostelry or roadside public house known as the Eagle and Child. This house was framed with timber, had projecting gables, and was altogether a picture of old age, and at last became so ruinous that about 1851 it had to be taken down, and the present Temple Hotel was built in its place.
>
> To this house there was a bowling green attached from time immemorial, and was probably as old as the house itself, which by appearance would be nearly three hundred years old.[64]
>
> It was on this green on August 17th 1819, that Samuel Bamford and a few coadjutors lunched off cold veal and ham, a part of what should have been their previous day's dinner, if they had not been so roughly handle and dispersed by the yeomanry.'[65]

Sam Bamford himself, in his autobiography, has this description:

> 'On arriving at the head of Smedley Lane, before descending past Smedley Hall, we met two men with a covered basket, and they asked us to go with them. They had got a good lump of a nice leg of roast veal, and some ham to match it, and were going to the Temple bowling green to meet some friends, and to discuss their grievances and their viand over a bottle or two of porter. We went with them, and met half a dozen others, and a discussion ensued on the state of affairs and of the course that should be taken by the reformers.'[66]

---

[63] Demolished

[64] That would mean it was built around 1550

[65] Manchester Streets and Manchester Men, T. Swindells

[66] Passages in the Life of a Radical, Samuel Bamford

Bamford, in using the name The Temple Bowling Green, shows that for many years prior to the pub of that name being built, the area and the surrounding properties had been known as Temple.

THE CRUMPSALL HOTEL – Public House[67]

The Crumpsall Hotel stood on the corner of Cheetham Hill Road and Tyson Street. Originally this was an impressive building in the traditional pub style but, in the 1970s, Holt's Brewery replaced it with a much less impressive edifice built of stock brick and with a flat roof

THE GEORGE HOTEL – Public House

Just a couple of doors further along from The Crumpsall was the tiny George Hotel. This pub fronted straight onto the pavement and was squeezed between a sweet shop and Titanic's delicatessen shop.

It boasted a thriving football team and the photo here (courtesy of Marie Conway) shows the men of the pub prior to setting off for a day at the races in the 1970s.

Just off the main road, on Arlington Street were two more street-corner pubs, The Joiners Arms and The Rising Sun.

THE HALF WAY HOUSE – Public House[68]

Situated at the junction of Cheetham Hill Road and Middleton Road there have been two pubs by that name on the same site. The first, stood close to where the White Smithy had previously been, facing onto Cheetham Hill Road.

It is believed that the original pub was built by the Phoenix Brewery, based in Heywood, but, as can be seen by the second photograph, the later incarnation was part of the Cornbrook chain. In its latter years it was a Wilson's House.

---

[67] Both old and new Crumpsall Hotels have been demolished

[68] Now the offices of a firm of solicitors

York Street

THE HALF WAY HOUSE IN 1927 AND IN 1970

THE ROBIN HOOD HOTEL – Public House[69]

Formerly known as The Shooting Butt and Bowling Green, and later just The Butts, this was the preferred meeting place of the local archers, whose practise ground stood behind the pub. Close by the pub was the shop of Mr. Pilkington, the bowmaker and fletcher.

Although the Cheetham Archers were fortunate to count James Rawson among their number, it was not thought fitting to name the pub in his honour.

Considering that it was built almost at the time Rawson died, to name it after him would have been a fitting tribute to this great sportsman and would have gone a long way to immortalising his name and his prowess as a bowman.

At one time a central feature of the social life of Cheetham Village, the pub had a chequered career and gradually declined to such an extent that it was considered, by many residents, to be an unsafe place to visit.

THE ROBIN HOOD HOTEL IN A STATE OF DECAY

It had a brief resurgence under the name Ferdowski, but that ultimately failed and, after lying empty for several years, it has now been converted into two fast food takeaway outlets.

THE DERBY BREWERY ARMS – FORMERLY THE KNOWSLEY HOTEL – Public House

The Knowsley Hotel was previously a Whitbread House, but it was acquired by Holts and became the Derby Brewery Arms and, as such, the 'Brewery Tap' for Holts, whose Derby Brewery sits immediately behind it on Knowsley Street.

It is now also the training centre for Holts and the upstairs is equipped to give all the necessary training for prospective tenants and landlords.

---

[69] Now sub-divided into two fast-food outlets

York Street

The pub appears to have been larger when it was first built but, for decades past, the right-hand side has been a separate concern, seeing usage as a shop and for other purposes over the years.

Notably, this is the building where the state of Israel was born. This was once the headquarters of the Manchester School of Zionism, founded by Chaim Weizmann.

The meeting between Chaim Weizmann and Arthur Balfour led to The Balfour Declaration which stated 'His Majesty's Government looks with much favour on the establishment in Palestine of a national home for the Jewish people'.

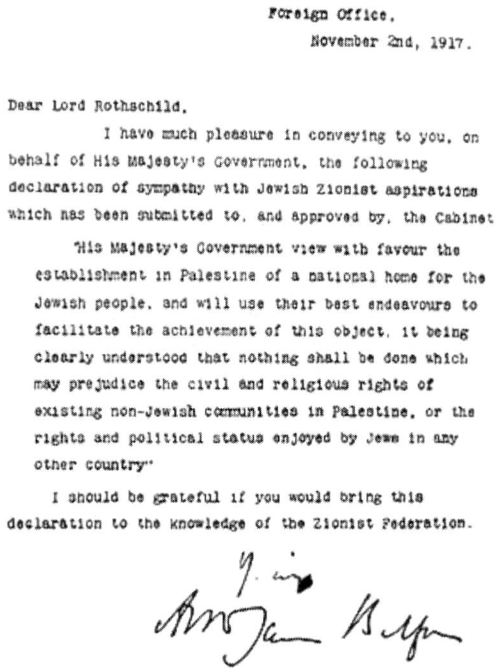

THE EMPRESS HOTEL – Public House[70]

Standing at the highest point of Cheetham Hill village The Empress has been a landmark on the skyline for approaching 200 years.

The name was originally The Bird in Hand and the present building replaced an earlier one, of the same name. Shortly after the visit of Queen Victoria and Prince Albert to Manchester in 1851, the pub was re-named The Empress, in recognition of her title 'Empress of India'. However, the fabric of the pub belies the new name including, as it does, small carvings of a bird in a hand over the windows.

WINDOW SURROUNDS DEPICTING THE BIRD IN HAND

---

[70] Now sub-divided into small offices

York Street

THE PLEASANT INN – Public House[71]

This was surely the smallest pub on Cheetham Hill Road. A look at the map of 1900 will show that it extended more fully behind the frontage than the surrounding terraced houses and shops and the photograph shows that it was a full story higher and markedly better-built than the surrounding properties. Little else is known of this modest establishment.

UKRAINIAN CLUBS AND CULTURAL CENTRE

From the 1920s the Ukrainian Community began to develop its own infrastructure:

> 'Ukrainian Social Club [Український товариський клуб] – a community centre which served the Ukrainians who settled in Manchester before the Second World War.
>
> The club was established in 1929 through the efforts of Joseph Lesniowsky, a leading member of the pre-war Manchester Ukrainian community.
>
> Initially the club occupied a single rented floor at 116 Cheetham Hill Road.
>
> In 1933 it moved to rented rooms on one floor at 48 Cheetham Hill Road. In about 1943 new premises were purchased for the club at 188 Cheetham Hill Road.[72]  
>
> The club became the centre of the social and cultural life of the community, a venue for the celebration of religious feast days and the marking of national anniversaries.
>
> It had a bar which provided it with a financial base. In 1933 the club had 116 members. Although most were Ukrainian, a small number were Lithuanian, Jewish, English or Irish.
>
> During the Second World War the club was frequented by Ukrainians serving in the Canadian and US forces stationed in the United Kingdom, and by Ukrainians in the Polish Armed Forces under British command. It became a regular meeting place for members of the Ukrainian Canadian Servicemen's Association (UCSA) which was formed in Manchester in 1943.

---

[71] Demolished – now within the area known as The Green Quarter

[72] Now the site of Granmore Ceilings

In the immediate post-war years, the club continued to serve as a social and cultural centre for the large numbers of newly-arrived Ukrainians who began to settle in Manchester and the surrounding area.

After the Manchester branch of the Association of Ukrainians in Great Britain acquired its first community centre in 1951 the club declined in importance, though it continued to exist for several years.

In addition to Joseph Lesniowsky, other officials of the club included Peter Tarnawsky, Wasyl Solar and Wasyl Marchuk. In January 1943 the UCSA president Bohdan Panchuk was elected president of the club.'[73]

The building which is now the Ukrainian Cultural Centre at 31 Smedley Lane was bought in 1963. A hall was built shortly afterwards, by the efforts of the community, but this was, tragically, destroyed by a massive fire in February 2005. After a long and costly wrangle with insurance companies a new hall was built and the centre continues to be the main focus for Ukrainians in the Northwest of England. Check dates.

KOLO POLSKI, POLISH CLUB, CHEETHAM HILL ROAD – Private Members' Club[74]

The Polish Club was established in 1949 in a former private residence. In time, it was possible to add a two-storey extension behind the house giving two large halls which could be used for functions.

For a time, the lower hall functioned as a church, with a Polish celebrated there each Sunday.

Dwindling membership eventually resulted in the closure of the club in the early 2000s. The building is now a banqueting hall and function rooms.

THE HOUSE WHICH BECAME THE POLISH CLUB

---

[73] From the website www.ukrainiansintheuk.info/eng

[74] Now a restaurant

York Street

THE PREMIER PICTURE HALL

'This cinema was opened by 1915. It was operated by Circuit Cinemas Ltd. and, in 1925, they built and operated the new, much larger Premier Cinema (later ABC) across the road. The Premier Picture Hall was then re-named Greenhill Cinema (after nearby Greenhill Road).

The Greenhill Cinema was taken over by the Union Cinemas chain in the early 1930s and, by 1937, it was operated by an independent.

The Greenhill Cinema was closed on 19th May 1962 with Gregory Peck in "The Guns of Navarone". It was converted into a bingo club, which operated for many years. Since that closed, the building has become a supermarket, named Manchester Super Store.'[75]

Contributed by Ken Roe

THE PREMIER CINEMA

'The Premier Cinema was built for the independent Circuit Cinemas Ltd. and opened on 3rd August 1925 with Norma Shearer in "Excuse Me". It was taken over by the Associated British Cinemas (ABC) chain on 21st January 1929.

This large suburban cinema billed itself as 'A City Cinema in the Suburbs'. It had seating provided for 1,287 in stalls and 600 in the circle. The lower parts of the auditorium walls were lined with Mahogany panels, while the upper parts had panels with a gold floral design. There was a 10 feet deep stage, and a large cafe on the first floor which was decorated in a Chinese style, and was for the use of patrons and non-patrons. It was re-named ABC in 1965, and was closed on 25th July 1970 with David Bradley in "Kes" and Christopher George in "The Thousand Plane Raid".'[76]

It was certainly considered 'state of the art' at the time it was built:

'A striking profession of faith in the cinema's future is embodied in the new Premier Cinema situated on Cheetham Hill Road which has been opened this week. Obviously, it needed a great deal of optimism and confidence on the part of the proprietors to build even in a large suburb, a picture theatre equal in many ways to the best that Manchester possesses.

The Premier Cinema is planned in the Neo-Greco style, executed in Christie stone and rustic facing bricks, and is without question an architectural gem. A large entrance hall is provided with a fine main staircase leading to the balcony, both being lighted by a stained-glass dome. There is ample space between each row of seats to allow late-comers to pass through without disturbing anyone.

Notable features of the theatre's equipment are its fine ventilation and heating systems and its admirable proscenium. A symphony orchestra of some dozen players has been engaged under Mr. Arthur Ward's direction and a bold policy of production intended to include the best and newest films of the day has been decided upon, so that in no respect will the premier prove inferior to the city cinemas.'[77]

In 1953 children from nearby schools were brought to the cinema to watch film of the Coronation of Queen Elizabeth II.

---

[75] www.cinematreasures.org

[76] www.cinematreasures.org

[77] Manchester City News 8 August 1925

York Street

THE SNOOKER HALL AND CINEMA SIDE BY SIDE
(FROM THE COLLECTION OF ANDY ROBERTSON)

TEMPERANCE BILLIARD HALL

The building next door to the cinema (between it and Trinity Church) has a facade flanked by a tower on each side. Behind the façade is a curved roof with roof lights and, on each side of the doors, there is an impressive ceramic depiction of St. George and The Dragon.

This building was never a cinema. It was a Temperance Billiard Hall designed by architect Norman Evans around 1906. It remained in use as a snooker hall until the mid-1980s when it was also bought by Manchester Super Stores and was linked with the former cinema next door.

Manchester historian Andrew Simpson gives a little more information about the Temperance Halls:

> *'They were built by the Temperance Billiard Hall Co. Ltd which was founded in 1906, based in Pendleton. With an eye to a good site and, perhaps, a captive audience, some of the more enterprising early cinema owners chose to site their picture houses beside temperance halls. This was true of Chorlton and of Hyde Road.*

THE TEMPLE PICTORIUM

Despite the rather grand name it had when it opened, The Temple was considered by many to be the 'inferior' cinema of Cheetham Hill Road, often referred to (affectionately?) as The Flea Pit. Certainly, it never had the grandeur of The Premier or The Odeon, but it is fondly remembered, by many, as the home of the Saturday Matinee.

In its later years it developed a reputation for showing more X-rated horror and 'adult' films and this is reflected in its final offering in the week it closed:

> *'It opened as the Temple Pictorium in November 1913. The Kinematograph Year Book 1914 lists the Temple Picturedrome on Cheetham Hill Road with a capacity of 1,250. The owner is I. E. Morrison. In 1937 it is styled the Temple Pictorium, seating 844, with BTH sound and with a 14ft deep stage and two dressing rooms. The owners are Temple Pictorium (Manchester) Ltd. and it was operated by the H.D. Moorhouse Circuit.*
>
> *In 1954 seating had fallen to 782. The proscenium was 30ft wide with a 15ft screen. The owners are the same. By 1963 it was operated by the G.B. Snape Group of Assoc. Cinema Companies chain. In the summer of 1972, it was twinned by splitting the auditorium down the middle. It closed on 28th December 1983 with 'Krull' and 'Sex in a Women's prison'.*

Contributed by H. J. Hill

York Street

THE ODEON CINEMA

'The Riviera Cinema-de-Luxe stood on Cheetham Hill, near its junction with Elizabeth Street.

Originally due to be named King George Cinema, it opened on 14th May 1931 with "Paramount on Parade", plus a gigantic variety show on its stage. It was operated by the J.F. Emery Circuit, but only for one year. By 1935 it had been re-named Riviera Cinema. In 1937 the proprietor was Anglo Scottish Theatres Ltd. of 2 Cavendish Square, London. Capacity is given as 2,117 with 1,625 in the stalls and 492 in the circle. It was equipped with a Western Electric sound system. The stage was 18ft deep with 4 dressing rooms.

In June 1938 it was acquired by the Odeon chain and given that name on 2nd October 1944. By the time of its closure on 4th March 1961 capacity was 1,974. Its final films were Kenneth Moore in "Man on the Moon" and "Marriage of Convenience".

It was gutted internally and converted into a 10-pin bowling alley which opened on 21st August 1961 as the Top Rank Bowl (Top Rank being then owned by the Odeon chain). It was sold on 9th July 1971 to Rayburn Trading who operated within the building.'[78]

Contributed by H. J. Hill

Later in the 1970s the building was destroyed by a huge fire, which took hold on a Sunday afternoon, thankfully, when nobody was on the premises. At the height of the blaze, the roof collapsed and aerosol cans, were fired into the air like rockets by the ferocity of the heat.

The photograph here shows the cinema, not long after it closed in 1972. The advertisement for the coming of the Ten Pin Bowling alley can be seen to the right of the picture.

The bowling alley was relatively popular for about ten years.

THE GLOBE CINEMA

The Globe Cinema stood, just off Cheetham Hill Road, on Thomas Street, opposite the Wesleyan Cemetery.

The cinema was part of a chain, the H.D. Moorhouse Circuit, which was built up over several years by Moorhouse, who successfully bought up a number of independent cinemas across Greater Manchester and beyond.

THE SHAKESPEARE CINEMA

The Shakespeare Cinema was a building very similar in design and size to the original Premier Picture Hall and, surprisingly, stood no more than 100 yards from it, which meant that, after the new Premier was built, there were three picture houses within a stone's throw of each other. Clearly, the people of the area in those days had a large appetite for filmgoing.

---

[78] www.cinematreasures.org

York Street

After its life as a cinema, the Shakespeare was one of the very first supermarkets to open in North Manchester. It was strange to walk between the shelving on the sloping floor where the seats had once been.

THIS MAP SHOWS THE CONCENTRATION OF PLACES OF ENTERTAINMENT AROUND GREENHILL ROAD

THE BIJOU PICTURE THEATRE

Few people nowadays will recall this little cinema which existed on Cheetham Hill Road from the earliest days of the last century until at least the time of the Second World War, although precise dates have proved elusive to find.

It was the brainchild of a Welshman who combined cinema and theatre in a uniquely 'Cheetham Hill' form:

> *'Most early cinemas, whether they had been converted from theatres or purpose-built, had at least a small stage in front of the screen. Local cinema operators could be highly inventive in presenting non-filmic attractions to draw on local audiences.*
>
> *Perhaps most idiosyncratic, however, were the theatrical performances offered alongside screenings at Manchester's Bijou Picture Theatre in the Cheetham Hill Road. Located a short distance from the imposing Great Synagogue in a heavily Jewish neighbourhood, the Bijou was a small, family-run affair with seating for three hundred that catered to the local community. Listing in the 1914 Kinematograph Yearbook reveal the venue's proprietor to be Arthur Cheetham, a pioneering Welsh film-maker that turned to cinema ownership later in his career, acquiring several interests in Manchester.*
>
> *Interviewed as part of a project recording the social history of Jewish Manchester, organised by the historian Bill Williams, respondent Joe Philips recalled the Bijou being run by a Mr. Fischer (presumably managing the site as an employee of Cheetham). Fischer, according to Joe, was an experienced and passionate actor from the Yiddish stage, and it was these talents he brought to his role as cinema manager, putting on playlets in Yiddish for his predominantly Jewish audience. As Joe recalls:*
>
> "In between films he would put on sketches, and they were very good – well produced, well-acted. He took a leading role. They lasted about 20 minutes, half an hour. I spoke Yiddish and, naturally, I liked them. I enjoyed them." *(Manchester Jewish Museum Archive).*
>
> *Marshalling family and friends into supporting roles, Fischer's cinema was an intimately local space juxtaposing recognisable faces from the immediate neighbourhood with international film stars in an innovative form of cine-variety; unsurprisingly Joe thought the attraction "unique".*

York Street

The Bijou, stated Joe, was his favourite cinema and he remembered a heterogeneous audience comprised of children and adults of all generations – in this blending of entertainment forms all apparently found something of appeal'[79]

In the photograph The Bijou is the building with the arched windows in the centre. Beyond it is the Great Synagogue. Far from being 'a short distance' away it was right next door.

THE MAJESTIC ROLLER-SKATING RINK

Tucked away on Thomas Street, next door to the Globe Cinema was the Majestic Roller-Skating Rink which enjoyed huge popularity during its heyday.

It boasted two skating sessions each day and even a full band to accompany the skaters in the evenings.

Skating clubs also used the facilities, and competition for places was keen.

Both the Globe and the roller rink were demolished in the redevelopment of the area and the site they occupied is now covered by the Cheetham Shopping Precinct.

FINNIGAN'S DANCE HALL AND ACADEMY

Just next to the Queen's Road Bus Depot for many years, stood Finnegan's Dance Hall and School of Dancing. It stood in what had originally been the garden of a large house and consisted of a simple building with a corrugated iron roof but with a fancy façade facing the main road.

It was the favourite meeting place for generations of young men and women from as early as the 1930s.

The evenings there would be divided into two parts. The first, was the teaching part, where experienced dancers were employed to coach newcomers in the intricacies of the waltz, the foxtrot and the quickstep.

---

[79] Jews, Cinema and Public Life in Interwar Britain, Gil Toffell 2018

The second part would be for 'free dancing' where the latest trends such as the Charleston, the Jitterbug and later the Jive and the Twist could be enjoyed by old hands and beginners together.

In the summer of 2006, after standing closed for some years the end came when the hall was destroyed by fire. The Manchester Evening News was inundated by readers' letters, giving their fond recollections of the establishment:

> 'A fire that destroyed one of Manchester's most famous dance halls has prompted a flood of calls from Advertiser readers keen to share their memories.
>
> The home of Finnigan's, on Queen's Road, Cheetham Hill, was gutted when flames ripped through the building last week.
>
> The dance academy taught ballroom dancing to generations and served as a meeting place for hundreds of marriages.
>
> Established in 1877 by James Finnigan it was one of the country's oldest dance schools when it closed in November last year. Throughout its history it was run by the Finnigan family, passing to James's daughters Ethel Kerrigan and Cissy Ryder before passing to his granddaughter Joan, who ran it with husband Frank for 66 years. They continued teaching there into their 80s but sold up last year and moved to Chadderton.
>
> The couple's daughter Julie, who moved to London in 1978, was among those to get in touch. She explained she had followed in the footsteps of her parents, who were North of England champions, as an accomplished competitor in Latin American dancing.
>
> She said: "It was very upsetting to find out what had happened. Whenever I come to visit mum and dad I always drive past the place and it was sad to see it in such a bad way even before the fire. I was there from being a young girl and, like my three brothers, was involved in helping in the cloakrooms and the pay box and later I taught dancing. I remember there being hundreds of people coming in even on the one night and they came from every walk of life imaginable."
>
> Many others told us it had been a fundamental part of their youth and all agreed it was sad to see the legacy come to an end.'[80]

THE DEMOLITION OF FINNEGAN'S 2006

THE ICE PALACE, DERBY STREET

It is hard to believe, but Cheetham Hill once hosted a World Sporting Championship:

> 'Opened by Lord Lytton on October 25 1910, clad in white marble, The Ice Palace, as it was known, hosted the National Ice-Skating Championships a year later and the World Ice Skating Championships in 1922.
>
> At the end of each day, the churned ice from the rink was pumped through an underground pipe to ice works, in a building across the road. Fresh iced water was then pumped back to refresh the rink's surface overnight.
>
> The Ice Palace was the only ice hockey rink in Britain during the early 1920s. A game between The Army and 'The Rest' was played at the Ice Palace in November 1923 to select the British team for the 1924 Winter Olympics.

---

[80] Manchester Evening News and Advertiser

It was closed in 1915 and used to manufacture observation balloons for the war effort. It reopened on November 21, 1919. It was requisitioned by the Ministry of Aircraft Production in 1941 and later reopened as an ice rink on March 21, 1947.'

When it finally closed again it was used as a milk bottling depot and later a snooker hall. Famously, and sadly, in the declining years of his career, former World Snooker Champion Alex 'Hurricane' Higgins could be found there playing anyone who was willing for £10 a frame.

CHEETHAM WAKES

Wakes were, and in some places still are, annual holidays observed by the workforce of an entire town at the same time.

Particularly popular in mill towns, these took place in rotation, between June and September. They allowed for maintenance to be carried out on all the machinery at the same time and ensured that the mill was always staffed to capacity the other 51 weeks of the year. The practice continued in these districts long after they had faded from use elsewhere.

It was common for travelling fairs to visit each town in turn 'following the wakes' around the country and these fairs would attract huge throngs to their cheap, colourful entertainment.

The earliest mention of wakes in Cheetham Hill dates from 1877. In March of that year the Home Secretary had issued an order that the wakes fairs should be abolished. It is not clear why this step had been taken, but it was, in some places, strongly resisted, or simply ignored. This report comes from the Bolton Evening News of 25th August of that year:

> *'Ist. August, 1876. It being the anniversary of what were called "Cheetham Hill Wakes," two defendants, along with numbers of others, obtained possession of a field abutting on the Hill-road, and there, erected shows, shooting galleries, swing boats, photographic tents etc, together with other surroundings of a fair.*
>
> *There were complaints from the inhabitants of the neighbourhood soon as it was established. Inspector Atkinson said he visited the place and found the defendants in the occupation of the shows etc.'*

The two men, in their defence, pointed out that the words of the ban were "in any thoroughfare or strait." And that, since the fair had been erected on a private field, the law did not apply. The case was adjourned for two weeks to allow consideration, during which time the fair was unable to go ahead. The outcome of the case is not reported but, suffice it to say, more than a decade later the fair was described in these terms:

> *'No fair in Manchester is better kept than the old Cheetham - hill Wakes. The excellently planned fair ground has been crowded to its utmost capacity every night of the fair, and all did good business.*
>
> *The list of shows included: - R. Sedgwick's menagerie and series of living pictures; Alf Williams's phantoscope and war and other pictures; Dyer's dramatic sketch and Cinematograph exhibition; Professor Garland with his legerdemain and ventriloquism; Hughes's school of boxers and Mrs Hughes's up-to-date peep-show.*
>
> *A splendid set of Venetian gondolas is owned by the ground lessee, Mr. John Whiting. The big boat, Massey's and Kirby's swings, Chaplain's and B. Dixon's miniature horses, Hurst's Kaffir circus, and George Walker's steam horses were freely patronised.'* [81]

The location of the grounds where the fair was held is not given in any of the newspaper reports, except to say it was 'abutting the Hill road' and 'adjacent to Red Bank'. By a process of elimination this suggests the fair may well have been held on what is now the permanent site of the Manchester Showman's Guild at the end of Cullingham Street, off North Street.

---

[81] The Era – Saturday 18th August 1900

York Street

This was easily access by a footpath from Cheetham Hill Road, another from Queens Road and a footbridge over the railway from Collyhurst.

It would make perfect sense, historically, for a site used for a large annual event to be eventually bought as a permanent location.

York Street

CHAPTER VIII - MISCELLANY

CHEETWOOD - AN URBAN VILLAGE

Tucked into the bend between Cheetham Hill Road and Waterloo Road stands Cheetwood. It is hard to imagine, up until the mid-19th century, there existed here a garden village which was the place of resort for most of the inhabitants of the Cheetham Hill Road area. Once again, we have T. Swindells to thanks for his excellent description:

> *'The title urban village is apparently a contradictory one, but I think I can show that as applied to Cheetwood it is quite correct.*
>
> *To the visitor of to-day the place has not the charm that it had for our grandfathers, but it remains yet a little community standing by itself. It is, in reality, a village in a town. From the heights of Cheetwood you look down upon the surrounding town, and from no part of the village can the view be described as picturesque. Brick crofts monopolise the view on the one side, whilst in the direction of the Bury New Road the outlook is over rows of uninteresting houses, whose blue slate roofs and smoking Chimneys are a poor substitute for the expanse of gardens and fields that met the eye sixty years ago.*
>
> *In those days, although brick making had made its appearance in the vicinity, Cheetwood was a pleasant place to live in. The tea gardens, which were about midway through the village, was a popular place of resort in summer times. Loving couples would on Sundays and other holidays find their way thither, there to enjoy to a modified degree the pleasures of country life. Tea could be partaken of in the little summer houses that were dotted up and down the gardens, which were gay with numberless flowers; and the air was sweet with the perfume of roses, pinks, carnations, mignonette, and other blooms.*
>
> *At midsummer the smell of new mown hay was wafted from the adjoining fields, and in the autumn the sight of golden grain waving in the breeze met the eye. In the orchards the currant and gooseberry trees bore many a fine crop of fruit; and when the summer was on the wane the overhanging branches of pear and apple trees offered abundant temptation to the juveniles of the hamlet.*
>
> *A number of the houses stand in the midst of fairly extensive gardens, and others boast of a small patch of ground at the front. In contra-distinction from present-day custom there is no attempt at uniformity so far as the houses are concerned. Some of them appear as though they had been built in miniature. The entrances are low, and three storeys do not reach to a greater height than do two in more modern structures. The windows are filled with small panes of glass, and over many of the front doors are erected porches which in summer are usually covered with creepers. The architects of several of the houses have given a castellated appearance to the buildings by the erection of turrets and in front of one may be seen a number of pillars quite in the Grecian style. Certainly, the pillars support an iron balcony and the whole has a somewhat grimy appearance.*
>
> *Overhead there is a respectable show of foliage, which in summertime, in spite of the smoke-laden atmosphere, gives a pleasant relief to the eye. Although the atmospheric conditions are against the cultivation of the finer varieties of plants, many of the commoner flowers flourish and many a garden is gay with colour. Vegetables seem to flourish and a few years ago I saw a crop of oats growing in a small field there. The licensed houses in the village are quite in keeping with their neighbours. Up to the present no brewer has thought it necessary to erect one of those gaudy glaring buildings to be found in every other part of the City. They are 'plain and unpretentious', and provide facilities for their patrons to indulge in skittles and quoits.*
>
> *What the future may have in store for Cheetwood is uncertain. The advance of brickmaking may result in the gradual removal of the two hills on which it is built or failing that, some speculative builder may secure a portion of the land, pull down the houses, and cover the site of houses and gardens alike with rows of cottages. Then the municipal authorities may see fit to pave the village street and the few secondary lanes.'*

This description brings to life what the area must have been like in the middle part of the nineteenth century.

The 1857 map of Cheetwood shows in incredible detail all the small market gardens that proliferated throughout the area.

York Street

At this time, surrounding Cheetwood was nothing but open, uncultivated land but within its bounds could be found dozens of tightly-packed gardens producing vegetables and fruit, and providing a delightful place for people to take a walk in the summer.

Within another 30 years the entirety of Cheetwood Village had disappeared. The voracious brickworks had overtaken the entire area and not one stone was left upon another of what had been such a peaceful haven. Swindells' prophecy was proved

CAR SHOWROOMS AND GARAGES

From time to time over the last 100 years, companies have been established to cater for the motorist. From the earliest days of car ownership, showrooms have plied their wares to the people of Cheetham Hill Road.

Initially, carriage works, such as those on Seymour Road (later the base for the Mr. Whippy Ice Cream Company) were converted to deal with motorised transport and later, purpose-built garages and showrooms started to appear.

One of the earliest of these was the small garage on the corner of Seymour Road (now a restaurant). This picture shows the premises as they appeared in 1934.

This was also a petrol station, but it is just possible to glimpse the headlight of a car inside the building, designed with large, arched windows, to show off the vehicles to their best advantage.

Note, also, the flower beds in front of the building.

From time to time some large companies had their premises on Cheetham Hill Road, the largest of these being Kennings Ltd., on the corner of New Elizabeth Street, and Rosenfield & Henley's, which occupied a large part of where is now the Manchester Fort Shopping Centre, adjacent to Kennings.

York Street

Closer to Manchester, where there is now a snooker hall was William Arnold's showroom, shown here when Cheetham Hill Road was a much quieter place to drive, and a roundabout was sufficient to control the traffic at what is now a very busy junction.

Some older readers will still remember the Paramount Garages which pre-dated Wm. Arnold. This is a rather grainy image, taken from the opposite side of Ducie Bridge.

POLICE STATION

As is the way in the twenty first century, there is no local police station in Cheetham Hill, the nearest being at Harpurhey.

In former times there was a small police station on Humphrey Street, which boasted a 'lockup' for any felons who might need custody and a kennel for any stray or dangerous dogs which might be disrupting the peace of the residents.

This was replaced by a more up-to-date station on the main road, near the corner of Grangeforth Road. This, in time, became an 'unmanned' station, with an emergency call box outside and eventually even that facility was removed, the premises now being a 'Community Point' Resource Centre.

Perhaps it is the advent of mobile phones which has made local police stations redundant – it has certainly done much to remove telephone boxes from our streets.

York Street

HOTELS

Cheetham Hill Road has been well-served with small, low-priced hotels. Sadly, some of these developed reputations for being less than salubrious and, despite the best efforts of the owners, they have never thrived. In later years at least one such hotel was taken over by the local authorities to provide emergency accommodation for victims of domestic violence, and those who had lost their homes through eviction etc.

In the second half of the last century there were a few small hotels offering accommodation for travelling salesmen, visitors, businessmen and such. The oldest image here is of the Commercial Hotel which stood next to the Knowsley Hotel (later the Derby Brewery Arms). Millers Hotel stood adjacent to The Rally Club, one of the Ukrainian Clubs which have existed at various times along the road.

COMMERCIAL, CRESTA AND REGENTS HOTELS

BOOKS FEATURING CHEETHAM HILL ROAD

MAGNOLIA STREET – Louis Golding Novel

'Magnolia Street is rather like two later books, Howard Spring's Manchester saga, Fame is the Spur, and Walter Greenwood's Love on the Dole (set in Salford), in that it has a large cast of characters, mostly presented in a Dickensian way, with each of them given some striking and memorable characteristics, so that we remember each of them as their stories weave together.

But where the crucial topic of Spring and Greenwood is class relations, Golding's key subject is race. Magnolia Street is in a working-class district in North Manchester. One side of the street (the odd numbers) is Jewish, while the even-numbered houses are inhabited by gentiles. The novel follows the fortunes of the street's residents from 1910 to 1930.

Apparently, Magnolia Street is closely based on Sycamore Street, where Golding grew up, in Hightown, near Cheetham Hill, a district whose Jewish community had increased during the nineteenth century. (Sycamore Street was demolished in the slum clearances of the 1960s).' [82]

---

[82] Book review by George 'S'

York Street

THE MAISIE MOSCOE SERIES

ALMONDS AND RAISINS / SCATTERED SEED / CHILDREN'S CHILDREN / OUT OF THE ASHES / A NEW BEGINNING

This series traces the story of two Jewish families arriving in Manchester from Russia, through the generations. Set largely in the Strangeways and Cheetham Hill area they evoke a good sense of the history of the Jewish Community:

> 'A family's survival depends on their unbreakable bond…
>
> The Sandberg family arrive in England having fled Russia to avoid persecution. It is 1905, and in their new home of Manchester they soon discover that hardships can come in many forms. It's a friendship with their neighbours, the Moritz family, that finally makes them feel at ease.
>
> As the two families become increasingly intertwined, it is eldest son David who finds the culture of his new country encourages him to rebel against his mother's wishes. Sarah Sandberg has ruled the family with a quiet authority but now faces the challenge of a son who wants to shake off duty in his own desire for love and freedom.
>
> In the years ahead, the Sandbergs will face even greater challenges. It is only their enduring spirit that sees them overcome the odds to find sanctity, and even joy, as they survive each twist and turn of life.'[83]
>
> 'The first in the series is about a Jewish family who flee Eastern Europe in the early 20th century and settle in Manchester, England.
>
> In the cold world of Manchester in 1905 the family Sandberg found the good things of life scarce and the hardships bitter as the chill northern winds.
>
> Sarah, the mother. A born survivor stranded in a land of strangers by the vicious tides of persecution.
>
> David, the eldest son. Growing to manhood in a new world and torn between the clear-cut lines of duty and his own driving ambition.
>
> Through the Great War and the Depression, through the first fears of darker years to come, the Sandbergs reach out for the bitter and the sweet of life, the almonds and the raisins.'[84]

THE BILLY HOPKINS BOOKS

TOMMY'S WORLD / KATE'S STORY / OUR KID / HIGH HOPES / GOING PLACES AMYTHING GOES / WHATEVER NEXT[85]

These books are set largely in Collyhurst and Cheetham Hill and will appeal to anyone with an interest in either of those suburbs. They evoke the history of north Manchester and weave fact with fiction in the telling of Billy's family story:

> 'Tommy Hopkins was born in October 1886 in Collyhurst, one of the poorer, inner-city suburbs of Manchester. His father had quite a good job and there wasn't a lot of money to spare but Tommy remembered the home as being filled with love and laughter. He was an only child but thought that he was spoilt in terms of affection rather than in the form of worldly goods.

---

[83] Amazon review

[84] 'A Good Read' review

[85] The author Billy' Hopkins' suggested reading order

York Street

All that was to change when his father died of spinal meningitis and he and his mother had to move into cheaper lodgings. Even that tenuous security wasn't to last for long – his mother died of a heart attack in her thirties, leaving Tommy an orphan before he was eight years old.

Tommy's World is the lightly fictionalised story of the life of the author's father. It's been built up from stories that Tommy told his son over a pint in the local pub and whilst Billy Hopkins can't vouch for the accuracy of the stories he was told and some characters are composites in the interests of making a better story it is essentially a biography of his father's early life. It's the seventh book which the author has written on similar themes but it can easily be read as a stand-alone and if you were planning on reading more than one Hopkins advises that this might well be a good place to start.'

THE MONKEY RUN

In the period between the wars, it was common practice for the young men and women of Cheetham and surrounding areas to take part in a social ritual known as The Monkey Run.

This was a way of 'eyeing up' the members of the opposite sex when it was not considered seemly to be too close together unchaperoned. On a Sunday evening, the 'boys and girls' would walk up and down each side of The Village, meeting, greeting and chatting, and occasionally, perhaps, even flirting.

No doubt there would be plenty of comments exchanged between the parties at a safe distance, and it was all 'good clean fun'.

Some years ago, these two poems were printed in the Manchester Evening News on the subject. Sadly, nothing more is known about them other than the names of the authors:

THE MONKEY RUN
Where are the folk we used to meet on The Village long ago
The friends who used to smile and greet us with a bright hello?
Where now are the carefree boys, the happy, laughing girls,
Tommy with the foghorn voice and Joan of the golden curls?

>   *Along The Village regularly as Sunday nights came round*
>   *Crowds of people leisurely paraded up and down*
>   *Old folks enjoying the evening air, shining Village 'blades'*
>   *All spruced up and debonair like guardsmen on parade*

Harry, Des, Billy, Reg and lots of other fellows
So awfully genteel and 'Alderley Edge' with their bowlers and umbrellas
Territorials proud and smart, sailors home from sea
Trim young maids from Broughton Park and lads like you and me

>   *No loud transistor sets were heard, no stereophonic blast*
>   *Or caterwauling group disturbed our Sundays in the past*
>   *Only Tommy's raucous shout, and Bob's ear-splitting yell*
>   *That brought the landlord storming out of the Robin Hood Hotel*

York Street

Many a Darby met his Joan here, many a Jill her Jack
And old companions now far from home perhaps, sometimes, think back
With a deep nostalgic sigh, remembering the fun
We used to have in days gone by along The Monkey Run.

J. Kelly

A short while later a reply was published in the paper.

UP THE VILLAGE
Reading of The Monkey Run in good old Cheetham Hill
Where many a Darby met his Joan and many a Jack his Jill
Reminded me of days gone by, especially in the thirties
When lads and girls like you and I enjoyed their weekend 'flirties'
Remember all you wallas of The Globe in Thomas Street
The Majestic Roller-Skating Rink, where regularly we'd meet
A tanner at the back, mi' lads, and threepence at the front
Bing and Bob and Fred Astaire would do their latest stunt
Falling in 'Mug's Alley' while the others skated round
Having to be sorted out and picked up from the ground

> *Lorenzini's corner where the pop and ice-cream flowed*
> *Tiger nuts and Monkey nuts and shells all down the road*
> *Liquorice licks and swaggering sticks, and Uncle Joe's Mint Balls*
> *Mint Imperials, nugget bars and sometimes, best of all*
> *Lovely whipped cream walnuts bought from Meeson's down the road*
> *Five cigarettes with matches from the shop on Crescent Road*
> *How did we really do it on so little, and have such fun?*
> *For nowt at all, on Sunday night we'd walk the Monkey Run*
> *Up The Village on one side, then back along the other*
> *Meeting friends along the way and greeting one another*

Ankle-length for Sunday best, and pointed high-heel shoes
Pill-box hats and ankle straps were fashionable news
Hat and coat with dress to match, and shoes of sim'lar colour
Long scarf-collars wrapped around, with 'edge-to-edge in summer
And what about the local boys in suits of navy blue
Of brown and grey, their trousers creased with good, broad turnups too
Some wore trilbies, some wore pots, smart overcoats as well
In summer, open-necked white shirts, grey flannels, they looked swell
With smart, greased hair, so shortly-cut, clean-shaven were our gang
The girls with 'page-boys' at the back, and in the front 'a bang'

York Street

Then came 'the call' we answered, all, on land and sea and air
The L.A. and the N.A.A.F.I., the W.R.N.S. W.R.A.F. and A.T.S. were there
We'll meet again, we all said then, no matter, nor how long
Departed, smiling cheerfully, and sang a happy song
The black-out came, oh what a shame, it spoilt our Monkey Run
Where we had had such happy times, much pleasure, lots of fun
I wonder where they all are now, no doubt some ne-er came back
Yet we remember every one, when we start looking back
So, thank you for the mem'ry, though the years may come and go
Of the life we shared with many 'up The Village' long ago

CONCLUSION

This, then, is the far-from-complete history of an extraordinary district of an extraordinary city.

It is difficult, in a book of this size, to do more than scratch the surface of the whole story, but the history of Manchester can be found interwoven in the buildings and characters of Cheetham Hill Road.

From humble beginnings, at the confluence of two minor rivers, Manchester has grown to become a major player in world events, helping to shape the future of industry, science, commerce and the arts.

A quirk of geology raised the village of Cheetham Hill above its surroundings, allowing its inhabitants both a clear view, and clear air, and enabling them to forget, at least for a while, the squalor of the town which had created their wealth.

Generations of unfortunates and dreamers inhabited its streets and courts and began the process of creating the rich mix of culture and style which makes present day Cheetham Hill unique.

Future generations may take up the task of recording what happens next but for now this is 'the story so far'.

York Street

BIBLIOGRAPHY

Bamford, Sam	*Passages in the Life of a Radical*
Connell, Lisa	*The Ultimate Scapegoat: The Irish in England During the C19th*
Dobkin, Monty	*Broughton and Cheetham Hill in Regency and Victorian Times 1999*
Frangopulo, N.	*Rich Inheritance 1962*
Gittins, Martin	*A Crumpsall History 2020*
	St Chad's Manchester 1773 – 2006
	The Irk Valley from Manchester to Blackley 2021
	The Parish and The People 2005
Harris, Mike	*Up the Hill (Community Play)*
Harris, Ruth-Ann	*The Nearest Place that Wasn't Ireland*
Inglis, James	*Played in Manchester*
Streeter, Edwin	*Pearls and Pearling Life*
Swindells, T.	*Manchester Streets and Manchester Men 1905 – 1909*
Tait, J.	*Medieval Manchester and the Beginnings of Lancashire.*
Unknown	*The Cheetham Hill Circuit Jubilee (Wesleyan Methodists)*
Williams, Bill	*Migration Histories (Website)*
	Jewish Manchester, an Illustrated History
Wood, Robert	*Bowling and Bowling Greens*
Wroe, J.	*Peterloo Massacre, containing a faithful narrative... Edited by an Observer*

FACEBOOK PAGES

Did You Live in Cheetham or Cheetham Hill
Friends of St Mark's Cheetham
I Remember the Old Crumpsall
Manchester History
Manchestermasjid
Remembering Blackley
The Cheetham and Crumpsall Heritage Society

WEBSITES

All-things-considered.org
bfnda.org
cinematreasures.org
confidentials.com
Encyclopedia-titanica.org
Library.chethams.com
Manchester.gov.uk
manchesterhistory.net
manchesterjewishmuseum.com
www.manchestermasjidmotgm.uk
palgrave.com
togethertrustarchive.blogspot.com
ukrainiansintheuk.info
workhouses.org.uk

NEWSPAPER SOURCES

Manchester City News	*1925*
The Builder Magazine	*Various Dates*
The Era	*1900*
The Manchester Evening News	*Various Dates*
The Manchester Guardian	*1862*
The Manchester Times	*1872*
The Sphinx	*1879*

York Street

INDEX

A.W.N. Pugin, 25
Abraham Moss High School, 61
Absalom Watkins, 5, 6
Agricola, 1
Alderman J. Fitzimmons, 26
Alex 'Hurricane' Higgins, 80
Alms Hill, 2, 28, 29, 33, 36
Anchor Court, 59
Andrew Simpson, 75
Ardwick, 2, 10, 22, 44
Arlington Street, 69
Arthur Balfour, 71
Arthur Cheetham, 77
Ashley Lane, 5
Athenaeum, 20
Balfour Declaration, 46
Bar Mitzvah Boy, 11
Bedford Falls Publications, 3
Bellott Street, 62
Benny Rothman, 16
Bent Street, 63
Bignor Roman Villa, 3
Bignor Street, 3, 57
Bijou Picture Theatre, 77
Bill Williams, 63, 65, 66, 77
Billy Hopkins, 86
Bird in Hand, 8
Blue Coat School, 12
Borough Reeve, 6
Bowling Green, 6
Doyle Street, 34
Brideoak Street, 22
Brigantes, 1, 2
Brookfield, 3, 7
Broughton, 2
C. W. Ethelston, 51, 67
Castlefield, 1
Catterick, 1
Cavalry, 1
Chaim Weizmann, 71
Charles Dickens, 5, 10, 32, 52
Cheeryble Brothers, 32
Cheetham, 29
Cheetham Archers, 70
Cheetham Assembly Rooms, 25, 26, 67
Cheetham Baths, 29
Cheetham Branch Library, 28
Cheetham Central School, 61
Cheetham Congregational Church, 61
Cheetham Higher Grade School, 61
Cheetham Hill Conservative Club, 60
Cheetham Hill Town Hall, 24

Cheetham Hill Wakes, 80
Cheetham Hill Wesleyan Methodist Church, 59
Cheetham Reform Club, 57
Cheetham Shopping Precinct, 78
Cheetham Town Hall, 26, 67
Cheetwood School, 62
Chester, 1
Chetham Society, 20
Chetham's College, 1
Chetham's Library, 20, 21
Chethams Hospital, 41
Chevroth, 65
Circuit Cinemas Ltd, 74
Clarendon House, 23
Clinical Hospital for Women and Children, 29
College of Islamic Studies, 62
Collegiate Church, 11, 40, 41
Collyhurst, 6, 36, 59, 81, 86
Commercial Hotel, 85
Community Point Resource Centre, 84
Coronation of Queen Elizabeth II, 74
Coronation Street, 11
Councillor Daniel Boyle, 34
Crescent Road,, 8
Cross Street Chapel, 41
Crumpsall, 3, 8, 36
Crumpsall Hall, 8
Crumpsall Hotel, 69
David Loyd George, 33
Derby Brewery Arms, 24, 70, 85
Derby Street, 5
Dirty Lane, 2, 6
Don Ardern, 14
Dr. August Schoepf, 28
Dr. Turner, 20
Ducie Bridge, 5, 84
Ducie Wesleyan hapel, 58
E.W. Binney, 23
Eagle and Child, 2, 6, 68
Earl of Derby, 11, 52
Earl of Shaftesbury, 41
Eaton Road, 63
Ebenezer Chapel, 58
Edgar Allan Poe, 42
Edmund Salis Schwabe, 30
Educe Academy, 61
Edward Cockayne Chippindall, 38
Edward Loyd, 13
Elizabeth Gaskell, 12
Elizabeth Street, 2, 6, 56
Emperor Hadrian, 1
Empress of India, 71
Eustratio Ralli, 44
Falcon Villas, 8

Fallowfield, 10
Felix Mendelssohn, 52
Finnegan's Dance Hall and School of Dancing, 78
Fountain Street, 3
Fr. M. Sheehan, 57
Frances Eliza Hodgson, 15
Friedrich Engels, 2, 16
Friends of St Mark's, 52
George Condy, 42
George Cruikshank, 42
George Eliot, 12
George Hotel, 69
George Pilkington, 41
Gibralter, 5
Gilbert Winter, 6, 67
Granada Television, 11
Grangeforth Road, 84
Grant Brothers, 32
Great Cheetham Street, 2
Great Depression, 1
Green's Plan of Manchester and Salford, 31
Greenhill, 7, 13
Greenhill Cinema, 74
Grey Street, 63
Griffin, 7
Griffin Inn, 7
H. Green and Son, 32
H.D. Moorhouse Cinema Circuit, 75, 76
Half Way House Public House, 1
Halliwell Lane, 6, 7, 8, 12, 52
Halliwell Street, 62
Heath Street School, 61
Henshaw family, 7
Henshaw's School for the Blind, 12
Homes Fit for Heroes, 33
Honey Street, 58
Howard Jacobsen, 13
Humphrey Chetham, 8, 41
Humphrey Street, 8, 84
Hunt's Bank, 1, 5
Industrial Revolution, 1
Irk, 1
Irwell, 1
J. Tait, 1
J.F. Emery Circuit, 76
Jack Rosenthal, 11
James Crossley, 20, 32
James Rawson, 17, 70
James Stanley, 11
James Watt, 19
James Whitehead, 28
Jesse Fothergill, 12
Jewish Board of Guardians, 45
Jewish Heritage Committee, 66

John Brooks, 23
John Chippindall, 6, 37, 67
John Dee, 42
John Gregory Crace, 25
John Harland, 22, 23
John Rylands, 44
Joseph Abraham Hyman, 18
Joseph Lesniowsky, 72, 73
Joseph, John Thomson, 13
Joshua Brookes, 41
Kalooki Nights, 14
Kennings Ltd, 83
Knowsley Hotel, 85
Knowsley Street, 24, 70
Kolo Polski, Polish Club, 73
Laidlaw and Thompson, 58
Lancashire and Yorkshire Railway, 27
Lancaster, 1, 38
Leonard Kilbee Shaw, 64
Little Heaton School, 31
Liverpool and Manchester Railway, 6, 32
Liverpool Road, 6
London's Burning, 11
Long Millgate, 5
Lord John Manners, 41
Louis Golding, 85
M. Ainsworth, 4
Magnolia Street, 85
Maisie Moscoe, 86
Majestic Roller-Skating Rink, 78
Mamucium, 1
Man Booker Prize, 14
Manchester, 1
Manchester Carriage & Tramway Company, 34
Manchester Corporation Tramways Committee, 34
Manchester Education Committee, 20
Manchester Evening News, 30, 87
Manchester Fort Shopping Centre, 83
Manchester Free Gazette, 5
Manchester Free School, 11
Manchester Geographical Society, 20
Manchester Guardian, 26, 28
Manchester Hebrew Association, 62
Manchester Northern Hospital for Women and Children, 2
Manchester School of Zionism, 71
Manchester Showman's Guild, 80
Manchester Statistical Society, 20
Manchester Super Store, 74
Manchester Union Workhouse, 27
Manchester Victoria Jewish Hospital, 46
Mary Burns, 6
Mass Trespass of Kinder Scout, 16
Maureen Lipman, 11
Medlock, 1

York Street

Mendelssohn, 6
Messrs. Clegg and Knowles, 57
Mgr. Philip Hughes, 55
Middleton, 1, 8, 17
Middleton Road, 1, 8, 59, 69
Mile House, 31
Miller's Lane, 5
Millers Hotel, 85
Mills and Murgatroyd, 25
Moreton Street, 22
Mr John Pelter, 8
Mr T.W. Atkinson, 6
Mr. Fischer, 77
Mr. Gilbert Winter, 32
Mr. Halliwell, 7
Mr. L. Goodwin, 25
Mr. Pilkington, 8, 70
Mr. Thos. Henshaw, 7
Mr. Whippy Ice Cream Company, 83
Nathan Laski, 45
National Ice-Skating Championships, 79
New Bridge Street, 5, 27, 31, 60
New Elizabeth Street, 83
Newton Street, 44
Newtown, 10
Nicholas Nickleby, 10
Nobel Prize, 13
Norman Evans, 75
North Manchester Jamia Mosque, 62
North Street, 2, 6
O. Ashworth & Co, 30
Ordsall Hall, 42
Owens College, 13, 31
Ozzy Osbourne, 14, 15
Paramount Garages, 84
Parson Hey, 51
Peel Estate, 6
Pendleton, 2, 15
Pennines, 1
Peter Tarnawsky, 73
Peterloo, 42, 51, 67
Phoenix Brewery, 69
Police Courts, Minshull Street, 23
Police Station, 84
Polygon Road, 63
Premier Cinema, 74
Prestwich, 13, 17, 36
Prestwich Board of Guardians, 26
Priestnor Street, 6
Qamaruzzaman Azmi, 62
Queen Victoria, 71
Queens Road, 34
Ralli Building, 45
Ralph Brideoake, 11

Red Bank, 2, 5, 10
Rev Charles Wickstead Ethelston, 8, 51
Rev. Canon Cecil Wray, 40
Rev. Casartelli, 20
Rev. Lewis Loyd, 13
Rev. Sarah Fletcher, 59
Rev. Thomas Maddocks, 55
Rev. William Turner, 55
Rev. Hugh Stowell, 39
Rhodes New Bleach Works, 30
Ribchester, 1, 3, 36
Richard Bramwell Taylor, 64
Richard Cobden, 22
River Irk, 2, 5, 10
Robin Hood, 8
Romans, 1
Rook Street, 55
Rosen Hallas Home, 64
Rosenfield Ltd. & Henley's, 83
Royal College of Music, 14
Royal School of Medicine, 28
Rycroft House, 30
S.S. Carpathia, 19
Samuel Bamford, 68
Samuel Schuster, 6
Sandy Lane, 8
Sephardi Synagogue, 66
Seymour Road, 30, 63, 83
Sharon Osbourne, 14, 15
Sir Edward Holt, 29
Sir Oswald Mosley, 16
Smedley, 2, 3, 4, 19, 24, 33, 54, 55, 60, 73
Smedley Bank, 10
Smedley Bank Special School, 55
Smedley Cottage, 36
Smedley Hall, 68
Smedley Hill, 41
Smedley House, 45, 46
Springfield, 3
St. Bede's College, 20
St. Luke's Church, 3, 6, 33, 36, 39, 52
St. Mary's Ukrainian Church, 59
St. Chad's church, 55
St. Mark's Cheetham, 8, 17, 51, 59
St. Thomas's, Lower Crumpsall, 59
Stocks House, 2, 5, 6, 20, 21, 32, 67
Stocks Street, 18, 56, 57
Stonewall, 7, 12, 13
Strangeways, 5
Strangeways Park, 31
T. Swindells, 1, 5, 36, 51
T. W. Atkinson, 52
T.T. Wilkinson, 22
Tacitus, 1

Temperance Billiard Hall, 75
Temple, 2, 3, 4, 6, 12
Temple Bar, 2, 12
Temple Bowling Green., 6
Temple Cottage, 6
Temple Hotel, 68
Temple House, 2, 3
Temple School, 54
Temple Square, 33
Ten Hours Bill, 41
The Addison Act, 33
The Anti-Corn Law League, 22, 23
The Balfour Declaration, 71
The Bird in Hand, 71
The Chetham Society, 22
The Duke of Wellington, 6
The Ecclesiological Society, 53
The Empress Hotel, 71
The Globe Cinema, 76
The Green Quarter, 63
The Griffin, 67
The Half Way House, 69, 70
The Ice Palace, 79
The Joiners Arms, 69
The Knowsley Hotel, 70
The Manchester Guardian, 22, 90
The Manchester Times, 22, 58, 90
The Monkey Run, 87, 88
The Northern Hospital, 28
The Odeon Cinema, 76
The Peterloo Massacre, 51
The Pleasant Inn, 63, 72
The Premier Picture Hall, 74
The Prestwich Union Offices, 26
The Queen's Arms, 58
The Rally Club, 85
The Riot Act, 51
The Rising Sun, 69
The Riviera Cinema-de-Luxe, 76
The Robin Hood Hotel, 70
The Royal Society, 23
The Secret Garden, 16
The Shakespeare Cinema, 76
The Shooting Butt and Bowling Green, 70
The Talmud Torah School, 63
The Temple, 2, 6
The Temple Bowling Green, 69
The Temple Pictorium, 75
The United Kingdom Islamic Mission., 61
The Victorian Society, 26
The Village, 87, 88, 89
The York Mail Coach, 1
Thomas Ainsworth,, 20, 41
Thomas Henshaw, 12, 13

Titanics, 19
Toll-house, 8
Top Rank Bowl, 76
Torah Street, 63
Transport Museum, 34
Trinity Church, 59
Trinity College, Cambridge, 13
Tyson Street, 69
Ukrainian Canadian Servicemen's Association, 72
Ukrainian Cultural Centre, 73
Ukrainian Greek Catholic Church, 59
University of Louvain, 20
Victoria Memorial Jewish Hospital, 19
Victoria Station, 1
Victoria Wesleyan Methodist Church, 57
Viviana Radcliffe, 42
W. Raby, 44
Warrington, 1
Wasyl Marchuk, 73
Wasyl Solar, 73
Water Troughs, 8
Wellfield, 3
Wheeler's Manchester Chronicle, 67
White Smithy, 8, 69
Whitefield, 13
William and Daniel Grant, 10
William Arnold's, 84
William Harrison Ainsworth, 4, 20, 37, 41
William Murdoch, 19
Wilton Polygon, 63
Wilton Terrace, 6
Winston Churchill, 46
Workhouse, 5
Workhouse Brow, 5
World Ice Skating Championships, 79
Yentl, 11
York, 1, 2, 5, 15
York Place, 5
York Street, 1, 5

LOCAL HISTORY BOOKS BY BEDFORD FALLS PUBLISHING

    From the Green – 1

    From the Green – 2

    From the Green – 3

    From the Green – 4

    From the Green – 5

    Away from The Green

    Crumpsall Chronicles

    Smedley, The Forgotten Suburb

    Life Everlasting

    A Crumpsall Childhood

    Mark Addy's Irwell

    St. Chad's Cheetham

    A Crumpsall History

AVAILABLE ONLINE AT:

https://www.all-things-considered.org/corner-shop-1